SIXTEEN D

THE STORY OF 1

SIXTEEN DRUMMERS – THE STORY OF **THE UNDECIDED**

SIXTEEN DRUMMERS
THE STORY OF **THE UNDECIDED**

Written by:

Johann Shepherd (Koe)

With contributions from:

Tim Baldwin
Steve Houldsworth
Scott Montgomery
Steve Tempest
Mark Tempest
Daniel Green
Luke Parker

Illustrations by: Rachel Hickerton
Cover Design by: Dean Baldwin

SIXTEEN DRUMMERS – THE STORY OF **THE UNDECIDED**

Rombald

First published in paperback in the United Kingdom
October 2024

Updated in November 2024 – to also include Kindle.

Copyright © Johann D Shepherd – 2024

www.rombaldpublishing.co.uk

~

Johann D Shepherd asserts the moral right to be identified as the author of this work.

The author and publishers have made all reasonable efforts to contact copyright holders for permission and apologise for any omissions or errors in the form of credits given. Corrections may be made to future printings.

~

The author would like to state that some of the vocabulary and quotes used in this book were directly influenced by one of his favourite writers, the late John Sullivan OBE.

~

All rights reserved. No part of this publication may be reproduced, stored in a retrieval system, or transmitted, in any form or by any means, electronic, mechanical, photocopying, recording or otherwise, without the author's or publishers' prior permission.

ISBN: 9798339365907

SIXTEEN DRUMMERS – THE STORY OF **THE UNDECIDED**

In loving memory of Sam Carlisle. See you on the other side.

SIXTEEN DRUMMERS – THE STORY OF **THE UNDECIDED**

CONTENTS

- FOREWORD ... 10
- PREFACE ... 12
- INTRODUCTION ... 14

CHAPTER 1 – HUMBLE BEGINNINGS

- SAM'S FLAT ... 19
- BUSKING ON MAIN STREET ... 24
- WHERE'S YOUR KEYBOARDIST? ... 29
- THE UNDECIDED WAS BORN ... 34
- LIMO'S HERE! ... 43
- PAPARAZZI ... 50

CHAPTER 2 – FINDING OUR FEET

- NIGHT NURSE ... 55
- NO ROOM TO SWING A PLECTRUM! ... 59
- WHERE'S YOUR BACKLINE? ... 65
- SPILT A CURRY DOWN MY BEST MATE'S TOP ... 70
- TUMBLEWEED ... 74
- THE LONGEST SET ... 78

CHAPTER 3 – STARTING TO GET SOMEWHERE

- UNDER NEW MANAGEMENT ... 85
- CHARABANC TO LIVERPOOL ... 90
- INITIATION TEST ... 102
- BETTER THAN BISCUITS ... 108
- YOU SHUT UP SAM! ... 113

- FLY POSTING IN LEEDS ... 124

PHOTO GALLERY

- DAGGY'S DIARY ... 146

CHAPTER 4 – ON A ROLL

- BROTHERLY LOVE ... 153
- A BENEFIT FOR KOSOVO ... 158
- PARTY AT THE MANOR ... 161
- RAVING BONKERS! ... 165
- MY GUITAR'S TURNED TO JELLY! ... 168
- HOSPITALITY ... 172

CHAPTER 5 – GIVE AND TAKE

- GRAND THEFT AUTO ... 191
- WORKING CLASS HEROES ... 195
- DRANK THE PLACE DRY ... 198
- PLUGGING AWAY ... 202
- TOUCH AND GO ... 208

CHAPTER 6 – THE LATER YEARS

- BEATS AND BARMINESS ... 213
- ANYONE FOR CRICKET? ... 218
- JULIE ... 222
- CASTLE CAPERS ... 225
- A FAREWELL TO BOB ... 229
- SEE YOU ON THE OTHER SIDE ... 233

APPENDICES

- AFTERWORD ... 241
- ON REFLECTION ... 243
- ACKNOWLEDGEMENTS ... 253
- DISCOGRAPHY ... 255
- GIGOGRAPHY ... 257
- SUPPORT BANDS ... 260
- GEAR ... 261
- INDEX ... 263

SIXTEEN DRUMMERS – THE STORY OF **THE UNDECIDED**

FOREWORD

The real story of rock 'n' roll is littered with broken dreams, broken guitar strings, and broken hearts. We get too used to the usual rags to riches narrative as a bunch of wild-eyed outsiders conquer the world, that we forget that for 99.9 percent of bands their musical adventure is doomed to failure and yet this is where the best stories lie. The crazy self-belief that sustains the neon lit midnight motorway service lifestyle, the micro peaks of the occasional radio play or review and the dogged self-belief that somehow someone will get it one day is as much part of the dream as a tumultuous million-dollar fallout. The best bands don't always get to the top and yet their gold-plated dream defies all logic. From broken town backgrounds, their high decibel dreams and armour-plated failure matter little as the anecdotes pile up, they live like vagabond Robin Hoods on route to the loot.

This book is about such a band called The Undecided who stumbled out of Keighley and stumbled back a few years later with their dreams undiminished. A book full of hilarious or frustrating tales. They even once insulted my jacket at an

Oasis mega gig in Bolton and lived to tell the tale! It was the same jacket that Joe Strummer once offered me a couple of grand for...maybe, like Joe, they should have understood that rock 'n' roll is also about the flash!

John Robb

PREFACE

I decided to write this book shortly after my father died in 2022. It was when I was taking care of his affairs and clearing out his home, I stumbled across a large scrapbook which contained a plethora of memorabilia from my old rock 'n' roll band, some of which I'd not seen for nearly 30 years, including posters, flyers, tickets, photographs, and many newspaper clippings. As I read through them, the memories started flooding back of all the songs we'd written and performed, the gigs and events that we attended, the crazy capers we all got up to, and above all, the friendships we made, many life-long and some that were sadly lost too soon.

I want to tell you the whole story as I remember it, with the odd bit of humour bundled in, so let us say my account is 95% accurate, with a 5% sprinkle of stardust or artistic licence if you prefer. It has taken hundreds of hours to get these memories onto paper, and it's been quite an experience writing my first book and a fun journey exploring my past. I hope you enjoy this book as much as I have enjoyed writing it.

Koe

SIXTEEN DRUMMERS – THE STORY OF **THE UNDECIDED**

INTRODUCTION

It was December 1994; I had not long turned 18 and had just returned from a little gig at the Sheffield University Octagon Centre that had blown me away, and my eardrums too! I had just witnessed a band that made me feel alive; and opened my mind to a new beginning, it felt like I was part of a new movement, and that something big was about to happen. The band I'd just been to see was Oasis. I had only recently gotten into them having just come out of what I can only describe as a musical void; a kind of musical coma in the aftermath of Kurt Cobain's death earlier that year and not knowing what I wanted to listen to. Back then, Nirvana was my favourite band, and I even had a ticket to their next gig, but sadly never got the chance to use it.

I woke up the next morning, with the shrill of the amps still ringing in my ears, it reminded me of the gig all over again, the swagger of the Gallagher brothers, the caught-in-the-headlights stare of Bonehead, Guigsy and McCarroll, the energy in their songs, the sweat pouring off their faces and the crowd jumping up and down. We were moshing like crazy, crushing each other onto the floor, but we loved it all the same. It all flooded back, and I thought to myself, right, I'm going to get myself a guitar and learn to play and hopefully one day, I'll get myself into a band and be a performer and do what Oasis does, and just fecking love it!

Fast forward a few years later and I'm about to play in a band in front of a packed-out Cavern Club in Liverpool, the prestigious home of The Beatles. This was crazy, how the hell am I playing here? I'd only just learned to play the bass guitar and was about to step out onto the most famous stage in the world with its colourful graffiti backdrop of all the great band names that had once graced it. The band I was now part of was The Undecided, an unlikely grouping of lads from the town of Keighley and the village of Haworth in West Yorkshire.

The Undecided comprises Lead Singer Tim Baldwin, a mate of mine from school and the local Haworth Football team, Rhythm Guitarist Steve 'Ste' Houldsworth a mate of Tim's from Long Lee, and Lead Guitarist Sam Carlisle, a mate of mine from knocking about in the local park in Haworth since we were kids. He was known as 'Singapore Sam', as he lived there before coming to the UK. Then there was me, 'Koe' on Bass Guitar, and we had a drummer! Well, we had many drummers along the way; sixteen in total! Some played at gigs, some provided support in the studio, one was on emergency standby, and others came and went from various band rehearsals. Here's a list of some of the drummers I can remember the names of:

Simon Cartwright, Joe Woodger, Chris Jackson, Luke Matthews, James Ackroyd (RIP), Gary 'Rocky' Dwyer*, Steve Smith, Lionel Skerratt, Carl Stipetic, Gregg Lewis, Daniel Green, and Luke Parker.

The following chapters explain how things unfolded over the next 16 years between 1995 and 2011, and where these drummers slotted into our band's journey.

*Gary Dwyer, formerly of The Teardrop Explodes, was our emergency drummer on standby if we ever needed him. It turned out we never did, but he did attend some of our gigs in Liverpool.

SIXTEEN DRUMMERS – THE STORY OF **THE UNDECIDED**

CHAPTER 1

HUMBLE BEGINNINGS

SAM'S FLAT

It was a beautiful summer's day back in 1995. The sunlight was that proper golden colour, the type you only seem to get in those salad-day memories, the kind that only existed back in the day before all the global warming kicked off big time. I was on my way to my mate's flat, located in a building called Rochester House, which resided above a shop on the famous cobbled Main Street of Haworth.

They had only recently moved in, and I was looking forward to seeing their new digs. After a short walk from home, I arrived at Rochester House. It didn't look too bad on the outside; the frontage was in keeping with the local architecture and blended into the Bronte landscape. But as soon as I opened the main door into the communal foyer, I was hit with the stench of overflowing bins and cat piss. It lay thick at the back of my throat and started a burning sensation in my nostrils.

Once I'd finished chewing the lovely bin bottom air, I made my way up a few floors via a winding staircase and then down a narrow corridor to get to the flat. "Knock, Knock" or should I say "Boom Bloody Boom" on the door, I had to bang hard due to the noise. The sound emanating from the flat was on an industrial level and the door was almost vibrating off its hinges. What the hell was going on in there!? "Boom, Boom", I knocked again hard on the door.

This time my knocking was heard. The door slowly opened a crack, and no sooner than open to 45 degrees, this humongous cloud of steam enveloped me. I couldn't see a fucking thing! All I could register was a heavy smell of detergent. As the door opened wider, the cloud seemed to evaporate just enough for me to start seeing a silhouette of someone, it was like that film 'The Fog'. "Is that you Sam?" I said, "Yeah, err, alright Koe, come on in". "What's going on Sam, what the hell are you doing in here?" I asked, as I entered the flat. I needed to waft my arms about vigorously to try and see where I was going. I edged in a little further, my eyes slowly adjusted to the environment, and I could start to see where all the noise was coming from. It was one of those old twin-tub washing machine contraptions that stood there in the middle of the kitchen floor, and it definitely had some mileage on it. It was billowing out tremendous amounts of steam and soap suds, whilst swishing around what looked like hot grey drain water. "It's wash day today Koe" shouted Sam, "I'll be with you in a bit, go see Monty, he's in the living room".

Monty aka 'Scott Montgomery' was and still is my best mate who I've known since I was a baby. He'd moved out of home at a young age and was now sharing the flat with Sam. I made my way into the living room. The first thing I noticed as I entered the room was this huge thorny bramble bush that had made its way into the flat via a crack in the window and had started to grow inwards and wind itself around the back of the sofa. Best not sit over there, I thought to myself. It was also pretty damn hot in the room, and as I turned around, I could see where the heat was coming from. Monty was bobbed down in front of one of those two-bar electric heaters, although only one bar was working, it was still kicking out a bit of heat. He had a potato on the end of a stick and was trying his best to cook it over the heater. "Ayup Johann lad, how's thee", "Not bad Monty, not bad" I replied.

SIXTEEN DRUMMERS – THE STORY OF **THE UNDECIDED**

Now, at this point in my life, I still lived at home with my parents. So, washing and cooking were all taken care of, though I knew in the deepest depths of my mind that this was not the best way to cook a spud. I reserved my judgement and continued my conversation with Monty on what the past few weeks' activities had brought. "Well, Sam and I are thinking of starting a band," said Monty, "a band, what sort of band," I replied, "Rock 'n' Roll", said Monty; "Sam can play the guitar pretty well and I'm going to sing". I chuckled to myself and thought good luck with that, I knew Sam could play guitar but wasn't too sure about Monty's singing.

About half an hour later, Sam had finished his washing. Monty then abandoned the potato on a stick idea and wrapped the spud in tin foil and wedged it on the heater's grill to try and slow cook it.* We all made our way up the cobbled road to our local pub, The Fleece Inn, to quaff some of the finest Timothy Taylor's ales, play a few frames of Pool, and talk about this new band idea.

*I later heard that when they returned to the flat that night, they found that the potato had cooked quite well and had half each for their supper.

BUSKING ON MAIN STREET

I'd eventually made a start at being a musician and got myself a guitar. I had bought it from my boss at work as he no longer had any use for it. It only cost me £40, it was a Washburn D15 dark wood, a late 80s model and was probably worth a lot more. I got some music books from my local guitar shop 'S.A.M Acoustics' in Keighley. S.A.M's was a great little shop, and over the years I'd bought multiple guitars and amps from the owner Martin (RIP) and his son Bob. If there was anything you needed to know about guitars, S.A.M's was the place to go.

I then spent the next few months after work sitting in my loft bedroom persistently twanging out songs as best I could from the music books I had purchased, which ranged from The Beatles and The Rolling Stones to Nirvana and Oasis. A little note to anyone starting out playing the guitar, it does take a while to get used to playing actual chords and changing between them, and it does sound fuzzy as you miss-press the strings and it does bloody hurt for a while on the tips of your fingers, but with a little bit of perseverance, it does start to flow and your fingers will eventually go numb. "OK I'll stop waffling".

Meanwhile, whilst I was suffering blisters on my fingers and wondering whether to chuck in the towel, Sam and Monty started jamming. Sam was playing guitar, and Monty was singing through a drainpipe to mimic the effect of a microphone. I didn't get to witness this by the way! Monty told me they started out practising in the back room of the local Community Centre in Haworth. He told Sam they could practice there for free as he knew the Caretaker who said it was ok to play there anytime. This, unfortunately, turned out to be a little bit of a porky, and when the Caretaker heard them causing a din at the other end of the hall, he stormed in effing and jeffing and proceeded to kick them out.

Just a few weeks later, Sam and Monty found another location to jam their music and ended up in a room in Bridgehouse Mill in Haworth, though this time it was kosher. They were also looking to recruit some additional musicians to join them. Monty was asking around for guitarists and bumped into an old school friend of ours Tim Baldwin and asked if he knew anyone, to which he mentioned his mate 'Ste' who had been learning to play guitar. So, Monty invited them up to their next practice at the mill where he introduced them to Sam, and away they went.

Sam and Ste hit it off with their jamming and complemented each other well, Sam on lead guitar and Ste on rhythm. On the weekends they started to do a bit of busking on Main Street in Haworth to try and earn a few beer tokens. It worked quite well for them. I recall Sam sat outside The Fleece Inn, busking away, playing his electric guitar through a small amplifier that he'd fashioned from a small cigarette packet, it was ingenious and sounded quite loud for such a tiny thing.

Several months later, I returned to Sam's flat for a few beers. When I got there, I was graced with the sound of guitars playing and someone singing, though it wasn't Monty's voice. As I entered the living room I was greeted by some familiar faces. There was Sam obvs, playing guitar, Ste playing another guitar, and the vocals came from none other than **Tim Baldwin.** Now, I wasn't expecting to see/hear Tim singing. Tim was one of the tough lads from school, tough at Footy, and in a fight too, so to see him singing aloud, I first thought this can't be true, Tim singing? and then thought aloud "Wow, this sounds really good!"

I sat in the only seat available and reclined into the brambles, whilst cracking open a tinny, to marvel at the spectacle; my mates playing some familiar songs. I joined in singing along to songs like 'Johnny B. Goode' by Chuck Berry, 'Start Me Up' by The Rolling Stones and 'La Bamba' by Ritchie Valens. They all sounded great. Sam said they would get a set of songs together and then try to book a gig somewhere as soon as they could. I on the other hand, still had a long way to go with my guitar playing and continued to practice at home, with the thought that one day I would join a band.

WHERE'S YOUR KEYBOARDIST?

We'd rolled into 1996, and I'd been invited to see Sam, Tim, and Ste's new band play at The Shoulder of Mutton pub in Thwaites Village, Keighley. I'd never been there before but was told it was usually a quiet pub that served beer at £1 a pint. That's right, back then beer was cheap compared to today, we would always try to find the cheapest pubs, and anywhere that was £1 a pint (or 50p at happy hour) was a bonus, if it had a pool table and Jukebox it was a double bonus, if it had a band playing then triple bonus, but a mate's band, priceless! I'm up for that, I thought, this will be a right laugh. I called for my mate Simon 'Simi' Waddington and mentioned the gig, he was up for it, so we bussed it down to town and then walked the rest of the way to The Shoulder of Mutton with a group of other mates.

When we arrived, we noticed a few microphones set up at one side of the room along with a couple of dodgy-looking amps. Then there was this keyboard on a stand, it looked like one of those cheap Casio or Yamaha keyboards that were only any use in demo mode, you know, the ones that you see Jilted John Shuttleworth play.

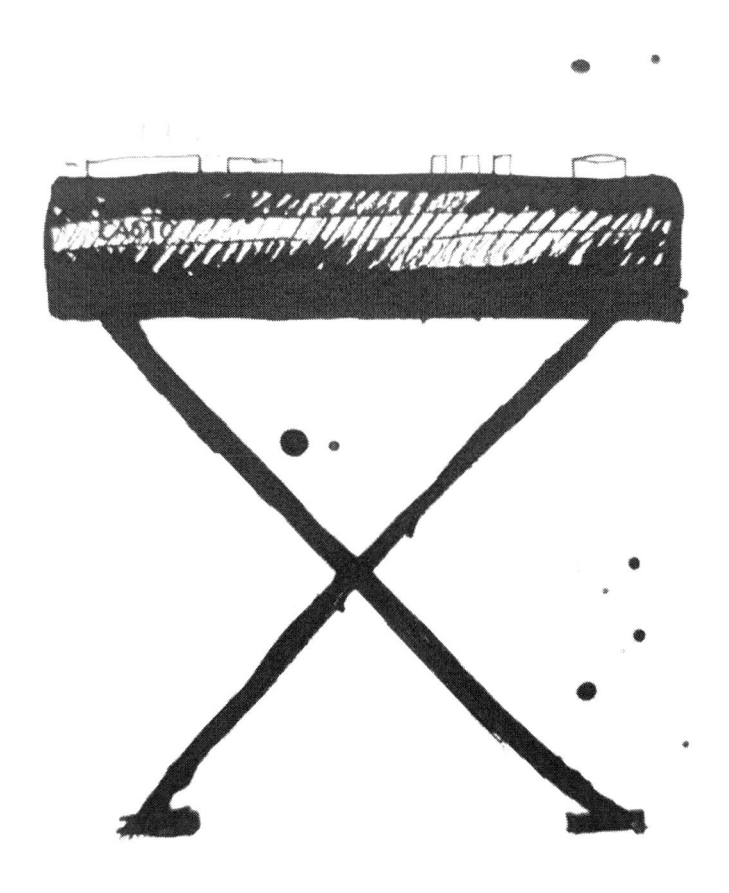

I wondered to myself who's playing keys?? So, I went to find Sam who was with Tim and Ste and a few other mates near the bar. "Where's your keyboardist?" I said, "Fuck knows" said Sam, "We've no idea where he's got to and we're on in 5 minutes". "Who is it then? I asked, "I didn't know you had anyone on the keys". "Baz Cooper" replied Tim, "He should have been here by now". Now, Baz didn't live too far away from the pub, pretty much across the road, so a search party went out to check if he was at home. They found him all right, he was crashed out on his sofa and had consumed too much exotic tobacco to be playing the keyboard. So, with that, Sam, Tim, and Ste had to play the gig without him.

The pub had started to get busy, and the beer-fuelled crowd started chanting and cheering to get the band on; the lads took to the stage. They started well considering they didn't have a drummer or keyboardist and got through a bunch of well-known covers. The crowd sang along. But as each song ended, Sam had a good swig of his favourite tipple, which consisted of Stella Artois with a lime top. By the time they had got halfway through the set, Sam was totally pissed, to the point that he was playing a different song to what Ste and Tim were playing. He ended up turning his back to the crowd and just went into a full-on lead guitar solo mode, playing whatever came to mind. I was pissing myself with laughter as nothing was in sync. Simi nudged me and said, "Hey Koe, you need to join this band mate, they need a bass player". "But I can't play bass, I've only just managed to get my head around playing the guitar", "Yeah, but it's easy to pick up if you can play guitar and you've got the fingers for it". "I'll have a think about it," I said, still chuckling away at what I was witnessing.

Then all of a sudden there was this almighty crash of a sound, KER JUNK!! In all the chaos, Sam had spun back around to face the crowd and ended up knocking his amp over. The reverb started to rattle away until someone from the crowd volunteered to help tip it back upright, but then the front fell off onto the floor; the speaker now facing down and muffled, had pretty much killed it. And that was the end of the lead guitar solos. But all was not lost, Sam unstrapped his guitar and staggered over to the keyboard that had been patiently sitting there all evening in standby mode, just waiting to be played. As soon as Sam sat behind it, I was wondering to myself how this was going to go down, what on Earth could he possibly play in that condition?

But Sam surprised everyone, he interlocked his fingers and stretched them out in front of him as if he was preparing to play on a Steinway Grand in front of a packed-out Albert Hall. He then performed a belter of a song and rescued the near-failing gig. It was 'Lady Madonna' by The Beatles, and he played it note for note perfectly, Tim singing and Ste playing along on guitar. The crowd all joined in, and they ended the gig on a high.

At that moment I decided to take Simi up on his advice and get a bass guitar, learn to play it, and join this band with no name. Even though what I'd witnessed seemed chaotic and unprofessional, I had seen their potential and it looked like great fun. I asked the lads if I could join as bassist if I learned how to play, they agreed, and with that, I went home happy with the knowledge that I would be joining a band with my mates. Bring it on!

THE UNDECIDED WAS BORN

It wasn't long before I got my new bass guitar, I'd popped down to S.A.M Acoustics and had a browse at what they had in stock. I was taken to a lovely-looking guitar that stood out from the rest, it was a Hofner-style Violin bass, like the one that Sir Paul McCartney played with The Beatles. I bought it on the spot, along with a little 50-watt practice amp. I spent the next few weeks learning how to play it, and in particular the bass tab parts to the songs I'd already learned to play on my acoustic guitar, along with some of the cover songs that Sam's band had played at their opening gig, so I could get myself ready to join them.

We all met up at Sam's flat to discuss the way forward. We soon discovered we were missing a couple of important things: a room to practice in and two; and most importantly, a drummer! "Does anyone know of any drummers?" said Ste. I knew of a couple from school, one of which was a mate. "Simon Cartwright," I said, "He can drum, I can ask him next time I'm in town, he works at 'Our Price', I can pop in and ask him". That weekend, I managed to recruit Simon who agreed to come and join us at our next rehearsal session, and Sam managed to find us somewhere to practice, which was upstairs above The Fleece in Haworth. We all met up there, set up all our music gear, got a few pints in, and started our first full band practice.

After a lot of debating on what to play, followed by lots of twanging, banging, and clanging about, we started to ease into a few covers to warm up. Ste also introduced a few originals into the mix, songs he'd penned whilst busking with Sam. Although the songs we played didn't sound polished in any way, *far from it,* we knew we had a rhythm and a beat, and it sounded ok. I was starting to feel confident with my bass and it took a couple of practice sessions before we had a set of songs in the bag.

"Shall I book us a gig?" said Ste, "I know somewhere we can play any time". "Where?" I replied. "At a pub called 'The Tap & Spile' in Harrogate" replied Ste; "OK let's go for it" we replied. But we then hit a bit of a dilemma! Simon had to bow out of playing drums as he couldn't spare the time to play in the band any further due to other commitments. And so, with that, we had to find another drummer, and quick! as we only had a week before the gig. Luckily, Ste managed to find a guy that he went to college with 'Joe Woodger', which was at very short notice, so much so, that we didn't even have a rehearsal with him.

We all turned up at the venue in Harrogate as a band with no name. Ste told Joe to keep a straight 4 beat to all our songs, look out for the changes and wing it as best he could. But after the first minute, we all sounded so out of kilter, it was like listening to a bunch of cuckoo clocks that were set to go off 5 seconds apart. We were all over the place. No disrespect to Joe, he did his best considering he'd not heard our songs before or even practised with us, but it just wasn't working. We had to resort to playing the rest of the set acoustically. Unfortunately, that was Joe's first and last gig, and with that, we were now without a drummer again, two drummers gone in a week! We started putting the word out again. We required a serious drummer who could play well, but also be reliable in turning up to both rehearsals and gigs.

We managed to attract the attention of someone who knew Tim's dad. He wanted to give his son 'Chris Jackson' a shot at playing with a band, and since we had nothing to lose, we agreed to take him on. After a couple of practice sessions, he was playing well with the band and started to gel. Then

Ste updated us, "We can play at the shoulder of Mutton again, we'll get paid and also have a bit of a rider!" We all looked at each other, wondering if we were gig-worthy yet, but that didn't matter one bit; getting paid and having a few free beers made our minds up all right, and we all agreed to do it.

So, Ste booked the gig for the following month. But there was one small issue still niggling at us, we didn't have a band name!? We headed back to Sam's flat and started to think of names, which to be honest, can be difficult when everyone starts to chuck in their two-pence worth. "Hey, what about this for an idea" said Sam, "there's an old sign from the shop below the flat in my storeroom, I'm not sure what it says, but maybe we could use it as the band name, and we could also use it as a backdrop at gigs". "OK then let's go get it, let's see what it says," said Ste.

Sam disappeared to have a rummage about in his storeroom and then swiftly reappeared dragging behind him several wooden boards back into the living room. When we pieced them all together, the sign read; 'The Bronte Footwear Company'. "Not exactly a band name," said Tim. "I'm not sure it has a ring to it" I concurred. "It was a good idea Sam, but not really the name for us," said Ste. "Oh well, fuck it" replied

Sam, "I've done my best, you lot will have to come up with a name then". So, with that, we all got our thinking caps on.

It was the night of the gig, and we all met up at the Shoulder of Mutton along with a few mates, including Monty. We'd still not agreed on a band name and all it said on the advertising blackboard outside the pub, was "Live band playing tonight". After much further debating, and not coming to any decision, Monty grabbed a piece of chalk from the barman, went outside and wiped off the words 'Live band' replacing them with 'Undecided' due to our indecision. "There you go lads, sorted," said Monty.

From that moment, as the punters started to arrive, they referred to our band as what it said on the blackboard and 'The Undecided' was born. The gig went well and due to a good turnout in the pub, the landlord paid us a bit more than was originally offered, which was most appreciated, and soon got spent behind the bar.

One of our next gigs was at a private do for a friend's 18th birthday party which was held at the Conservative Club in Wilsden near Bradford. All seemed to go well with our performance, and everything was going tickety-boo, that is until a bit of a fracas broke out and one of our mates; Chris 'Skoony' Myerscough had consumed one too many Sherbets and ended up throwing a hardened, curled-up egg sandwich across the room at someone, missed them, and ended up hitting a picture of the Queen and cracked the glazing. It shattered all over the floor*. It was us that ended up getting the blame, even though it wasn't anything to do with the band, though our drummer's dad wasn't too pleased with what he'd just witnessed and didn't want his young lad hanging around with a bunch of ruffians. That unfortunately ended Chris's career as the full-time drummer for The Undecided and was the last we ever saw of him.

SIXTEEN DRUMMERS – THE STORY OF **THE UNDECIDED**

A few weeks later, word of mouth for drummer number 4 had got out and about. A young lad 'Luke Matthews' turned up to our next rehearsal asking if he could audition for us and see how things go. We all agreed to give him a trial run and helped him lug his drum kit into the building. Having listened to Luke tune his drum kit for nearly 30 minutes of banging away like a game of Whack-a-mole, he was ready to roll. And BINGO! He was straight out of the blocks and on the ball for all our songs, great timing, bang-on changes, the lot. We were all properly pleased and offered him the role of our next stickman on the spot, and he agreed to join us. It was the fourth time lucky for us, and we'd found our drummer. The Undecided was now complete.

*The committee of the Wilsden Con Club were disgusted with what had happened, they wanted reimbursement for the damaged picture and threatened to ban parties and bands playing at the club in future. The thing was, the club had always been empty and losing money, and that night it was more packed than ever before, they took thousands over the bar. Ste told them to have a reality check, as they could now buy a hundred pictures of The Queen with the money that they had made that night and decorated the walls with them, Ste's comments weren't appreciated, though bands did play there again once some new blood had joined the committee.

LIMO'S HERE

We were barely into 1997 and had already booked about six or seven gigs, mainly local pubs and clubs and things were starting to look up. During one of our practice sessions, we were talking about what we'd been doing throughout the day as we all had day jobs. Sam had mentioned that he'd been doing some labouring work for this fella called Geoff who lived in Oxenhope, and that he owned a big white stretch limousine. "How do you fancy turning up to gigs in it" said Sam, and without hesitation we replied, "Yeah that would be well ace! Make it happen". So, the next day Sam asked Geoff if we could use his limo for turning up to gigs and he said "Yeah, no worries, call it £20 for each gig and I'll be there" replied Geoff. So that was the wheels sorted.

At the next rehearsal, we started to plan how we would turn up to the next gig in the limo, where would get picked up from, and then where we would get dropped off. Our next gig was to be held at The Druids Arms in Long Lee near Keighley. We also planned on some other little added extras for the gig to make it a bit more fun, and kind of quirky. The band all agreed it would be a good idea to purchase some daft clothes from a charity shop to wear whilst performing, a kind of wacky disguise. So, we all rocked up to Sue Ryder's charity shop in Haworth and started to rifle through the clothes rails. Sam was in first and managed to find a cool psychedelic 1970s Paisley shirt. Ste found a flowery shirt which I'm sure he still wears to this day. Tim picked up a long navy-blue Mac, the kind a flasher would wear, and Luke got a silk snooker player's waistcoat. I was last in and found this posh brown corduroy jockey's blazer with elbow patches, it looked like it had been donated by Princess Anne. Right, that's our wardrobe sorted.

Then we thought, what else can we do? "Right", said Ste, "let's ask the landlord Mick at the Druids if we can use his big projector screen behind where we would be setting up the PA and amps, and have a video playing during the gig". "Great idea! I said, "But what video shall we have?" "PORN" shouted Sam; LAUGHS from all around, "No Sam we can't have a porno video playing, it's my local pub, and my mum and dad will be there too," said Tim. "We could have a cartoon playing", said Ste, "I think my kid brother Sam has some cartoons on DVD, what about Scooby Doo, I think he's got that". "Let's go with that before Sam has any more bright ideas," said Tim. We all agreed to have Scooby Doo. That's the backdrop sorted.

It was the night of the gig, and we all met up at the Fleece in Haworth. It was pretty busy, with the sound of pool balls thwacking into each other to a backdrop of The Verve and Oasis tunes banging out of the jukebox at full volume. Many of our mates were there, all in good spirits as they'd either won their Saturday Football game or Cricket match. My mate 'Ben Furness' asked if we were playing a gig tonight. I said, "Yeah, we've got a gig at The Druids Arms in Long Lee, we'll be on in an hour or so". "You better get your skates on then" said Ben, "the taxis are busy tonight". "No need for a taxi", I said "We've got a limo picking us up", "Yeah, right," replied Ben.

No sooner than I said that someone came running into the pub shouting "Hey there's a big white limousine pulled up outside, wonder who that's for?" "Oh yeah that'll be for us," said Tim. We all downed our pints and cockily made our way to the limo like some kind of rock 'n' roll royalty. The chauffeur 'Geoff' got out and opened the door for us, he was dressed like Parker out of Thunderbirds. As I got inside, I noticed it was lit up with all kinds of multi-coloured lighting, it had sheepskin carpets like 5 inches deep, there was a minibar, buckets of champagne on ice, and loads of poshly wrapped sweets in the side pockets. "Fucking hell", I said, "we've hit the big time". A crowd had started to group around the limo. We wound down the windows, smiled the biggest widest grins and set off giving a two-fingered royal wave to the crowd and saying "Adios, see you at the gig".

As we approached The Druids Arms pub, we noticed that no one was outside. "SHIT" said Ste, "No one will see us arrive". "So, what!" said Sam. "Well, we've all chipped in for this limo, so let's at least be seen getting out of it". Tim, Luke, and I nodded and agreed that would be good. Ste spotted someone he knew exiting the pub, so wound down the window and asked him to go inside and tell everyone that a big limo was pulling up outside and it could be someone famous. "What, now?" said the fella. "No, not this minute" said Ste, "We'll go around the block again and be back in a few minutes". All agreed.

We set off for a whistle-stop tour of Long Lee, not the easiest of places to spin around a 14-foot-long car, and Geoff ended up driving us down a cul-de-sac. We ended up having to do a multi-point turn, 'Austin Powers' style to get back out onto the main road and time was ticking.

We eventually arrived back at The Druids Arms and pulled into the car park for a second time, and low and behold, we had our crowd, well kind of! It consisted of the guy that went into the pub to tell everyone, and about 3 other regulars, staring in anticipation as to who this was pulling up in the limo. "That's our crowd!" said Sam, "I've seen a bigger crowd in a telephone box". Accepted, we had pretty much been defeated on this one, we all got out, strutted into the bar, and recovered our pride with a pint.

The pub started to get busy, and we knew we had our whole entourage making their way over from The Fleece in Haworth. The clock struck 9 pm, and we were ready to rock. The pub was now heaving, packed to the rafters, and out we popped with our daft clothes on to a huge cheer and applause. With Scooby Doo on the backdrop, we went straight in with our most up-tempo songs, 'The Score', followed by 'The Girl', then 'Real World'. The place was bouncing with energy as we blasted through the rest of our songs, it was a faultless set, and we were on top of the world!

Afterwards, we all took the limo down into Keighley town and pulled up outside the Rat Trap nightclub. As the punters queued up outside to get in, we stepped out of the limo, half-cut and buzzing and somehow managed to jump the queue and get in for free, I think the bouncers thought we were real VIPs. The rest of the night was a blur, but I know we were dancing about like loonies for a good few hours, then went for a curry. I didn't get home until 4 am. A good day was had.

PAPARAZZI

We had arranged with our rehearsal room landlord Graham to play in his pub, The Fleece Inn in Haworth, as we'd always agreed to do a gig for him free of charge seeing that he allowed us to practice upstairs for free. This meant we'd not have to travel far or lug any gear around and could simply leave it set up after our practice session that week. That said, we did agree to use the limo again, which meant departing from somewhere other than The Fleece.

We decided to flip the journey we took last time and make The Druids Arms in Long Lee the pick-up point. We all met up in there and had a few beers with the regulars and it wasn't long before the limo arrived, and away we went, heading back to Haworth. On the way, we asked Geoff to drive us down the cobbled Main Street towards The Fleece so we could catch the attention of any locals out for a drink and act all rock 'n' roll star again. It was busy, and it took us a while trying to squeeze the limo past a crowd of tourists before we arrived at our destination.

SIXTEEN DRUMMERS – THE STORY OF **THE UNDECIDED**

SNAP

CLICK

As we got out of the limo, we ended up with cameras pointing in our faces, "It's the Paparazzi!" shouted Ste. Well, kind of, basically the 'Keighley News' and 'Telegraph & Argus' *. The local press had caught wind that we were playing the gig and would be turning up in a limo again, so they wanted to run a story on us. We all lined up in front of the limo as best we could, not exactly striking a pose, we probably looked more like a police line-up. After photos, we headed in, got a round of drinks, plugged in, and were ready to entertain. Just to explain the setup, the room we practised in had a split level. The back of the room where we had set up the amps and the drums were about two feet lower than the front where people would enter the room. This meant instead of us being level with the audience or better still, up on a stage, we were down in a pit with people looking down on us. It was weird to be playing to a crowd of mid-rifts, but we had to do this gig to keep the rehearsal room.

The crowd built up with a mix of pub regulars, a few tourists, and a bunch of our mates. We performed the same set as we did at our previous gig at The Druids Arms, and it went down well. Afterwards, a guy called Tim who was in the crowd approached us and offered to be our band manager as he saw potential in us. We even ended up going back to his house to discuss it further, but he just ended up getting intoxicated and completely forgot all about it. To be honest, we weren't ready for a manager just yet and thought it'd be too much hassle, so continued as we were and started to plan our next set of gigs.

*Over the years, we had a very good relationship with 'David Knights' from the Keighley News and 'David Barnett' or 'Simon Ashberry' from the Telegraph & Argus newspapers, and they helped promote our gigs and events to the local community.

CHAPTER 2
FINDING OUR FEET

NIGHT NURSE

We had now become well known for turning up to gigs in the limo and were featured in all the local newspapers. We had a gig booked at a Social Club in Harrogate which again required our trusty chauffeur Geoff to drive us there. It was probably the longest run out we had in the limo. We all met up again at The Fleece in Haworth, had a few swift liveners and headed off. Now this time, with the journey being that little bit longer than our usual trips out, and, with five bladders full of beer, we had no choice but to ask Geoff to pull over en route for a quick pee stop.

We all jumped out and lined up at the side of the road on the A59 overlooking the Menwith Hill Airforce base and proceeded to water the grass on the perimeter fence whilst staring out at some very large golf ball shaped buildings.

SIXTEEN DRUMMERS – THE STORY OF **THE UNDECIDED**

God knows what we looked like to passers-by all lined up pissing at the side of a limo, and it was a busy road. Then I noticed a security camera on the fence. "Oh shit", I said, "We're on CCTV, quick lads, zip up, we better get going". As we all shook up, Sam gave two fingers to the camera and we all bundled into the limo, "Quick Geoff" said Ste, "You better put your foot down". We sped off A-Team style as though being chased by Colonel Decker from the military police.

We eventually got to the venue and headed inside. It was already getting busy, mainly with young female nurses. Yes, that's right, it was a hospital social club. A group of our mates had also turned up including Keighley Albion Rugby League Team members who were mates with Tim. We strapped on our guitars and started to play. Some of our mates had already started to mosh about at the front of the stage and everything seemed to be going well, or so we thought!

We got about halfway through the set, then all hell broke loose. One of our mates, Barry 'Baz' Houldsworth*, decided it would be a good idea to jump onto Tim's back whilst he was singing, and then started swinging about on his neck doing his best to wind him up. But Tim was having none of it and just carried on singing and laughing at Baz who was now swinging from Tim's shoulder like some kind of crazed monkey.

Then, suddenly from the back of the room, the Rugby lads charged towards the stage, thinking that Tim was in some kind of trouble. He wasn't by the way, and we all knew that Baz was just dicking about, but the Rugby lads thought differently and dived in at Baz, disconnected him from Tim and were about to put him through a full scrum. We had to stop playing at this point and interject, as we knew Baz was on the cusp of getting a good hiding. Tim managed to calm the Rugby lads, letting them know that Baz was a mate and was just messing about. As the charged atmosphere simmered down, we continued the set and got huge applause at the end, not surprising, it's not every gig that you get that kind of foolery, but when you do it makes it even more memorable.

Afterwards, we all got invited back to a flat where some of the female student nurses lived. Yes, I know what you're thinking, and had a bit of an after party which then turned into an all-night stayover, yep that's right, and a very big headache the next morning. All I can say is whatever happens in a flat full of young female student nurses and a Rock 'n' Roll band, well... You can probably guess the rest!

*Turns out, Baz's wild antics that night was because he'd won a bottle of whiskey in the raffle held during the interlude, and he ended up necking it. Sam had also promised Baz that he could get up and sing 'Wish You Were Here' by Pink Floyd, but he was too far gone and instead resorted to monkeying about.

NO ROOM TO SWING A PLECTRUM

Sam had managed to get us a gig in Birkenhead, across the Mersey from Liverpool, at a place called The Victoria Lodge, 'Vicky' to the locals. This was the furthest we'd travelled with the band, so we had to head out earlier than usual. We all met up at the rehearsal room that afternoon and packed my van with all the music gear. Sam joined me in the van for the journey, while Tim and Ste cadged a lift with Tim's brother Dean and his girlfriend Heather in her car, along with her friend Michelle. Luke ended up making his own way there.

Now I'd not driven to Liverpool before, never mind Birkenhead, and this was in the days before Sat Nav, so we navigated the old-fashioned way by following the road signs. We got to Liverpool ok, but we then had to go through the Mersey tunnel to get to Birkenhead. Unfortunately, we ended up taking the wrong tunnel, the Kingsway Tunnel instead of the Queensway Tunnel. Sam and I thought we were in Birkenhead but instead found ourselves driving in circles around Wallasey. We stopped to ask for directions. "Where's Vicky" shouted Sam out of the window to an unsuspecting elderly lady at the side of the road. "Vicky who!?" she replied, "Vicky Lodge," said Sam. "I don't know her" replied the lady. "Eh, what's she on about Koe?". "She thinks we're asking for a person, not a place," I said. "Ah", "Where's the Victoria?" responded Sam. The lady pointed straight ahead. And so, we carried on driving up the road we were on only to find ourselves at the bleeding Victora Central Hospital!! Now finding ourselves completely lost, we traced our way back the way we came through the Kingsway Tunnel and into Liverpool. After another few wrong turns, we eventually found the entrance to the Queensway Tunnel and onwards to Birkenhead.

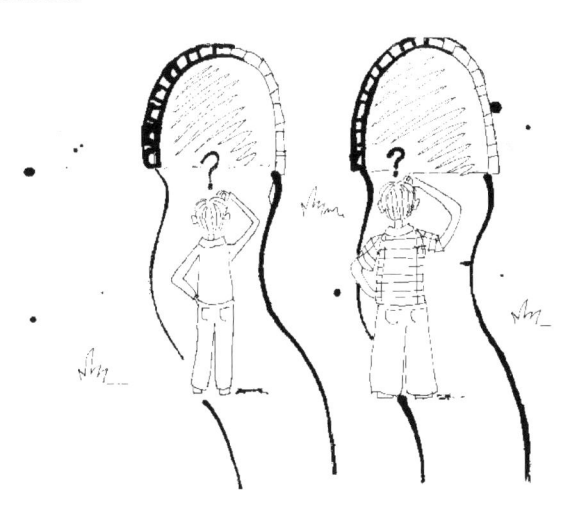

A few hours later and now starting to get dark we rolled up outside the Vicky Lodge, parked up and emptied the gear into the building. It was a strange place; a kind of back street hotel meets social club. It was somewhere that Sam knew from his past, as he'd lived just up the road when he was younger, and this became apparent when droves of people piled in and started hugging and greeting Sam as if he'd just returned home from a 10-year sabbatical in Oz. He introduced me to a few of them, including a guy called 'Nudge', who was quite a character.

I finished lugging all the gear in while Sam caught up with Nudge. Time was ticking and we were supposed to be playing soon but the rest of the band hadn't arrived yet. So, Sam started playing some songs on one of those upright pianos at the side of the stage area and entertained the folks. About an hour later, Tim and Ste arrived, but no Luke!? There was a pretty good crowd starting to build up which considering we'd never played there before was good, though it consisted mainly of a mix of local scousers, a group of elderly Irish folk that were staying at the lodge, and Sam's fan club. But still no Luke! We had to start the gig with no drummer, so we played all the songs we could do acoustically in the hope that

Luke would turn up soon. Then about halfway through our set, Luke appeared at the back of the room. "About bloody time" said Tim over the microphone. Luke sheepishly made his way to his drum kit and the crowd giving him a cheer along the way. With the full band now together, we started to rock with our usual set of favourite banger songs that got the crowd going.

After the gig we packed the van with the gear, the rest of the crew jumped into Heather's car, and we headed home. On our way back through Liverpool we needed to stop for fuel, so we all turned into the nearest filling station. I started filling the van with Diesel and on the pump in front of me, was Heather filling her car with fuel. I then noticed that something was pouring out of the bottom of her car onto the petrol station forecourt. I wasn't sure if it was fuel or not, but it was gushing out. It turned out the engine had a major leak, and all the oil had emptied out, leaving the car in a bad way and undrivable.

It was after midnight and with no breakdown cover, Heather had to call her dad to come and tow her home, this was to be a 3-hour round trip, and there was no way that we were all going to wait that long. So, we opened the back doors of my van and assessed what room we had left amongst the gear to fit people into. Ste and Luke managed to wedge themselves in between the drumkit and side walls of the van. Sam ended up being posted feet first into a small gap between the top of the amps and the ceiling. Tim did his best to try to get in but looking at what room remained, it would have been futile. "There's no room to swing a cat in here," he said. "There's no room to swing a plectrum," replied Sam. So, Tim got in the front passenger seat with his girlfriend Michelle sitting on his lap. Dean waited back with Heather for her dad.

We set off again, the van now much heavier than before, and you could tell, it felt spongy and unstable, so I drove as carefully as I could, trying to avoid any unwanted attention to the vehicle from the local bobbies. I headed towards the M62, then as we approached the beginning of the motorway, BLUE LIGHTS! "Oh Fuck!" "Everyone be quiet". A Police checkpoint had been set up and I'd just ambled right into it. This was the last thing I needed. An officer stood in front of the van. "Shit, he's got a gun," said Tim. It was armed Police. What the hell was going on? My bum was starting to squeak, I can tell you that for sure. I wound my window down. "Evening officer, what seems to be the problem" I said, as calmly as I could. "The motorway has been closed due to a situation*" replied the officer, "You'll have to find an alternative route". Now I wasn't going to ask any further questions, I just needed to bail out of this situation quickly before he noticed that I was way overloaded and carrying too many passengers. "OK," I said whilst winding the window back up and letting out a big sigh. "Phew!", "That was a close one". I spun the van around and headed in the opposite direction, checking in my wing mirrors to make sure I wasn't being tailed.

The Blue lights were now out of sight and not knowing which road to go down, as the M62 was the only road I knew would get us back home, I unintentionally headed south and ended up driving via Widnes before getting back to the M62 further down. I eventually got us back to West Yorkshire and dropped everyone off. I didn't get home until 04:30 am, I was totally knackered. What a bleeding palaver this evening has turned out to be, I thought to myself as my head hit the pillow and I started to nod off.

*We later found out that the motorway had been closed due to an IRA bomb scare following a bomb explosion at Leeds train station and various other locations earlier that day.

WHERE'S YOUR BACKLINE?

We'd been invited to play at Bradford's Centenary Music Week along with some other bands. It was a 5-day event, held at different venues across the city and our gig was to be at Queens Hall. We were quite excited about this as it was the first real music venue we'd get to play at, having only ever played in pubs and social clubs. We knew that bands such as Pearl Jam, Blur, Suede, Pulp, and The Cranberries to name a few had played there, so to us it was a big deal. We'd been given a bunch of tickets to sell by the promoter who was a crazy hippy wizard guy, and we'd managed to sell the lot, so we knew we'd have a full house.

We arranged for our trusty chauffeur Geoff to pick us up in the limo. Same old routine, pick up at the Fleece in Haworth. This time, with it being a real music venue, we thought we could just rock up a few minutes before our start time, get out of the limo to a crowd of people, swagger into the venue and plug and play. It kind of went to plan, all but the last part. When we got into the venue the stage was totally empty, no amps, or drums or anything!! We had entered the stage and were all ready to rock but had nothing to plug into and we were like WTF!! The promoter (Wizard) then collared us and asked, "Where's your backline?" "What do you mean, where's our backline?", we responded whilst scratching our heads. "Your amps mate, your drum kit etc" he replied. "Erm, we thought you were providing all that like, I'm sure you said it would be all laid on". "Nope! Only the PA, bass drum and stands". "You need to bring your amps and breakables" (cymbals/snare etc). FFS!! an obvious rookie error! What the hell are we going to do now?

The Wizard gave us an hour to get our gear, or we'd not be able to play. The problem was that all our gear was back at the rehearsal room at The Fleece pub in Haworth, which was just over 10 miles away. "Right lads, the limos already left, we've no wheels and, we need to get to Haworth and back within an hour, that's a 20-mile round trip through city traffic, so what are we going to do?" I said in a calm but panicking kind of tone. Everyone's faces went blank, but then out of the crowd, one of our mates Gareth 'Gaz' Evans* volunteered to give us a lift in his BMW. It made sense that I go with him, collect my van, then the gear and bring it all back, Ste also came to help. Now if you ever knew Gareth,

66

you'd know he was into his cars and was a keen driver, but I've never experienced a drive like it. He managed to whizz his way through the crazy traffic and get us to Haworth in less than 20 minutes, which was good going.

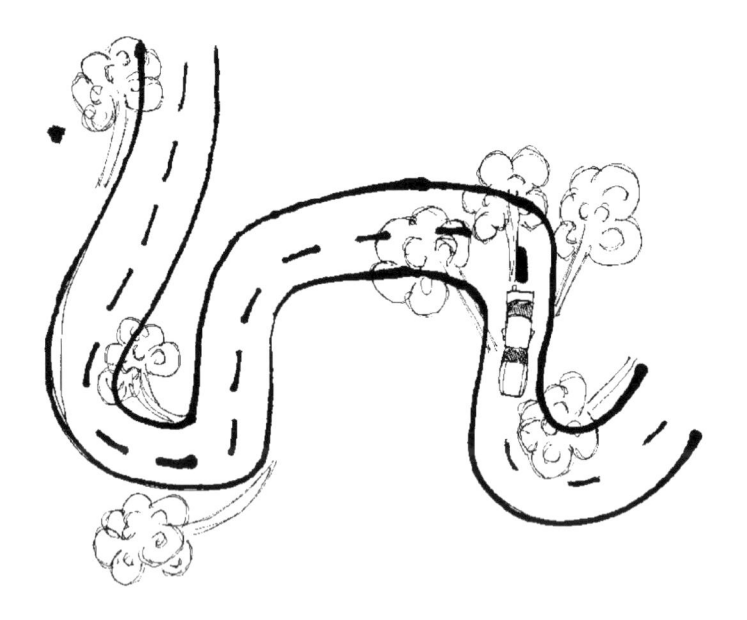

We screeched up outside my house. "Here, you go Koe, we'll meet you up at the Fleece and give you a hand with the gear", said Gareth, "Cheers Gaz, you're a star", I replied, as I sprung out of the car and then jumped into my van.

I whizzed up to The Fleece to get the gear, and on entering the pub, my sister Samantha who was the bar manager back then had to double take for a moment, "What the hell are you two doing back here, you left in that limo not long ago". "Tell me about it" I replied, we explained the situation and she chucked over the key to the upstairs practice room. Gaz helped me and Ste get the gear downstairs and into the van and we promptly whizzed back to Queens Hall, which took us a little longer than the journey with Gareth, but we managed to arrive there with 10 minutes on the clock.

We got the amps onto the stage and plugged in, as the crowd were all waiting on us. With no time to spare, we just went straight into the set, but due to all the mad rushing about we were all heavily out of tune, we must have sounded like a strangled cat on the first song. We all tuned up before the second song, but the nerves must have crept up on us, we were making mistakes left right and centre, which seemed to continue throughout the set. It wasn't our best performance by any means, but we still managed to get applause and some good feedback from the crowd and some of the other bands that were playing. But we knew we were bad that evening and chalked it up as a lesson learned and not to be repeated. Though if it weren't for Gaz, we'd have not even had the opportunity to play at Queens Hall, so good on him.

*Not long after writing this little story, I received some sad news that Gareth Evans had passed away just before Christmas 2023. RIP Gaz, say hello to Sam and see you on the other side.

SPILT A CURRY DOWN MY BEST MATE'S TOP

The time had come to make a recording of some of the original music we'd been practising, and we'd shortlisted four songs from our even shorter list. The first song was called '2am' and started with the lyrics, "Spilt a curry down my best mate's top". It was quite a funny song written by Ste and Tim about being on a night out on the tiles in the town of Keighley. After a skin full, down at the Red Pig pub on Church Green, they'd usually find themselves in the Rat Trap or Champers nightclub until the early hours before staggering and wobbling their way home and would often call in at one of the local curry houses en route. On more than one occasion they'd end up spilling most of their food down themselves or even someone else's clothes, and thus the lyrics were formed.

Second up was 'Happy Garden', the name originating from Ste's local Chinese takeaway. It sounds like a bit of a foodie theme coming along here but no, this one wasn't food related, it was just the title. **Next up was 'Brighter Day'. Ste wrote this with a view that one day things would get better than they currently were. Completing the 4-track EP, was**

'Real World' which could be a book within itself according to Ste.

We recorded the EP at Mill Studio in a place called Ickornshaw, it was near Cowling which wasn't too far from Keighley. We were practising there in a little room for a few months prior. We'd been asked to stop rehearsing above The Fleece due to us clashing with the Haworth Brass Band who were complaining that we were too noisy, and they couldn't hear their trumpets, we had no choice but to leave as they'd been practising next door for many years before us, and the landlord Graham didn't want the hassle. The guy who owned Mill Studio allowed us to record at a discount price, seeing that we'd been paying him to play in his practice room. This was all exciting to us, we'd never recorded before, and it started to seem like the band was becoming more and more professional now that we were in a studio.

We all set up our gear in this tiny little room and the recording engineer sat beyond a pane of glass in his little mixing booth. We pretty much rattled through the four songs, maybe recording each one three times, and picking the best to go into the master recording. To be honest, it wasn't the most polished production, quite raw, but we just wanted to hear what we sounded like. Afterwards, we were given a CD copy, and I went home to make more copies for the rest of the band. We were chuffed that we'd managed to record some music and decided to release it.

At the time we didn't have that much money between us to release it on Vinyl or even CD for that matter but were kindly offered the money required to have a small run of 100 Cassettes manufactured by the landlord 'Mick Baker' from The Druids Arms in Long Lee. He was a fan of our music and saw potential in us whilst playing at his pub. We managed to sell them all at gigs except a couple we kept for ourselves, although I'm not sure I have a copy anymore, they must be rare now. If you managed to get a copy, then keep hold of it, as Cassettes are making a comeback, and I think the 2am EP may be worth a bob or two one day.

TUMBLEWEED

It was the middle of summer 1997, and we had a good run of local gigs to do. First up was The King's Head in Keighley and we were supported by another local band called FIFA Guppy*. A bunch of our other old schoolmates also came to watch, which piled on a bit of peer pressure to put on a good show, which we did. I certainly believe that we must have inspired a few of them to start a band for themselves as the next time we saw them they were supporting us at some of our gigs the following year.

We also played a few more gigs at The Druids Arms, which had become our staple gig venue thanks to the landlord Mick, who always went out of his way to promote us, and we were always happy playing there every other month. The White Bear in Eastburn was another regular place for us. It was run by a couple of nice Indian ladies who looked after us. We often had a lock-in afterwards and they plied us with free drinks which included some amazing Long Island Tea's. The only downfall we had whilst playing at The White Bear was that they had this sound meter installed and we regularly tripped it out as we were too loud, meaning our PA and amps would switch off, leaving only Luke hammering away on the drums. We eventually managed to bypass the meter with a bit of crafty wiring and continued as loud as we could. Other gigs that summer were at 'Vicky's', which was part of the Victoria Hotel in Keighley, 'Robbos' which was a pub/club opposite The Shoulder of Mutton in Thwaites Brow, The British Legion in Haworth, which eventually became our HQ, and then we played a pub called The Punch Bowl in Silsden, just outside of Keighley, which was, let's say, one to forget, but I'll tell you all about it anyway.

We turned up to The Punch Bowl as we would with any other gig, though most of our gigs were on the weekends, this was a Wednesday evening. We set up our gear in the corner of the room. It looked all chintzy and floral with old brass ornaments dotted about on the windowsill, next to a few half-dead Spider plants that were poking through some dusty net curtains. You've got the picture, right? There was hardly anyone there, just a few locals propping up the bar, and a few in the tap room playing dominoes. Without any announcement, we started to play and just blasted out with 'The Score' which is the one from our repertoire that closely resembles a Sex Pistols song, all raw, shouty, and upbeat punk. We hadn't read the room properly. The few punters that were there at the beginning of the song, well, basically weren't there 3 minutes later when we'd finished it. Everyone had pretty much left the building. It was dead quiet and was a bit of a tumbleweed moment. The landlord came over, handed us £100 and told us to stop playing and leave. We were quite stunned by this but had no choice but to simply finish our beers and start packing our gear away.

As we were packing up, some of the punters started to come back into the pub, so Tim got up on the microphone and started singing the Frank Sinatra classic 'New York-New York' replacing the lyrics with "Silsden-Silsden" and then telling some jokes, which at first, got a few laughs, but as the jokes got bluer, the smiles soon disappeared. The barman came back over, unplugged the microphone, and told us all to "Fuck off and don't come back". So, we got the hell out of dodge with £100 on the hip and went to our friend Emma's** house to get pissed.

*FIFA Guppy was fronted by our mate Nick Chambers, who went on to become one of the founding members of the Beat-Herder music festival and invited us to play there in 2009. See Chapter 6, Beats and Barminess.

**Emma Baylin was Ste's girlfriend at the time. She was also the lead singer in a band called 'Surface' who supported us a few years later.

THE LONGEST SET

Having had a run of gigs throughout the summer of 97, we fast forward to autumn. Practising at the Mill Studio was taking its toll. Not only on the fact that it took ages to get there and back on an evening; but after picking everyone up and dropping them back off, it was costing us a pretty penny too. So, we needed to find somewhere closer to home and if possible, for free, like the arrangement we originally had at The Fleece. Sam mentioned this to his dad, Bob, who was a member of the local British Legion Club in Haworth and asked if he could help us out and see if they had any spare rooms in the building that we could use.

The next time Bob was having a drink at the Legion, he asked the landlord, 'Oggy' if we could practice upstairs. The thing was, on an evening, the upstairs was used for ballroom dancing for the 70+, so we had to get their permission to be able to practice there too, and we also had to become members; *of the Legion, not the 70+ dancing club.*

So, after a bit of negotiation between Bob and Oggy and meeting up with the Strictly crew, we ended up being able to get a couple of nights per week to rehearse there, on the condition that we provided them with free gigs throughout the year, which was fine with us, though one date they had in mind was coming up in the next few months, being New Year's Eve! The thing was, we felt that was a day that we should get paid as we'd normally be out with our mates celebrating and not wanting to work for free. So, we renegotiated with them, and asked to be paid £350, but all other gigs were for free, and they agreed, but with another final condition that we played all night on New Year's Eve.

"Have you enough songs in the bag to do all night lads?" said Bob. "Not at the moment?" replied Ste, "Don't worry Dad, we'll sort it," said Sam. We had our work cut out to get enough songs together for a whole evening and we needed to be tight on them all as it was going to be heaving and we were going to get paid royally. When I say royally, let me put this into perspective, £350 back in 1997 could get you approximately 230 pints of Guinness at The British Legion, in today's money with inflation and tax, that's around £1000!

We practiced like mad for the next few months on the run-up to Xmas and New Year and managed to get a good long set of songs together, which we ended up splitting into 3 sets to allow for a few comfort breaks in between; comfort meaning a piss and another pint.

Here's the actual set:

1. I Wanna Hold Your Hand – The Beatles
2. I Feel Fine – The Beatles
3. Twist & Shout – The Beatles
4. Happy Garden – The Undecided
5. Like a Dove – The Undecided
6. Absolute Madness – The Undecided
7. Roll with it – Oasis
8. Stand by me – Oasis
9. Supersonic – Oasis
10. Sandstorm – Cast
11. The Drugs Don't Work – The Verve
12. There She Goes – The La's
13. Real World – The Undecided
14. Brighter Day – The Undecided
15. Taxman – The Beatles
16. Come Together – The Beatles
17. Don't Let Me Down – The Beatles
18. 2am – The Undecided
19. Summer Song – The Undecided
20. Our Place – The Undecided
21. Talk Tonight – Oasis

22. Guiding Star – Cast
23. Alright - Cast
24. Brim Full of Asha – Cornershop
25. Start Me Up – The Rolling Stones
26. The Score – The Undecided
27. Day Tripper – The Beatles
28. Help – The Beatles
29. Sonnet – The Verve
30. Lucky Man – The Verve
31. Live Forever – Oasis
32. Married with Children – Oasis
33. Feeling Better – The Undecided

We then ran out of songs that we'd practiced to perfection, and the crowd, which was in the many hundreds, wanted more, so we had to repeat a good few more, totalling 40 songs. In all, we played for nearly 3 and a half hours. We were pouring with sweat after that, and I'd gone from drinking beer to ice water to cool down. It was a fantastic night, enjoyed by all and it tested us to the maximum of our capability then. But more was to come.

SIXTEEN DRUMMERS – THE STORY OF **THE UNDECIDED**

CHAPTER 3
STARTING TO GET SOMEWHERE

UNDER NEW MANAGEMENT

It was January 1998, and we started to reflect on the last couple of years, the gigs we'd played, how well things were going and wondered what we should do next. Tim brought his mate Steve Tempest or 'Tempo' to our next rehearsal to listen to us play, as he'd expressed an interest in the band and wanted to help us out. Tempo was a local lad from Long Lee and had known Tim and Ste for many years as they played cricket together for the local team. Tempo was a bit older than us and had a wealth of musical experience, he'd spent a lot of his years in the 1970s and 1980s living in Liverpool and working with many well-known Merseyside bands such as The Teardrop Explodes and Echo and The Bunnymen. He also hung around with the then young Courtney Love who spent her youth embracing the Liverpool punk scene.

One thing that Tempo had picked up on was that we were still very much a covers band, with the odd few original songs. "Why don't you ditch the covers and start writing more of your own music," said Tempo. "You'll get further as an original's band than a covers band". "I've got a load more songs written," said Ste, "and we could bring them into the set", "Yeah, I agree", I replied, "I've also been writing some songs, we could give those a go too". Tim, Sam, and Luke agreed it would give us something new to focus on.

We decided not to book any more gigs until the summer and spent the next few months learning the new songs. We all met up at The Legion for our next rehearsal and introduced the new songs into the set, which were, 'Our Place', 'Feeling Better', 'Like a Dove', 'Absolute Madness', 'Summer Song', 'Rose Above', 'Time', 'A Killer Amongst us', and 'A Million to One'. Although the last four songs were played a good number of times at our gigs, we unfortunately never recorded them, so they are truly lost in time.

Once we had become comfortable in playing the new songs together, we performed them to Tempo. "Fugkin yeh, youz'lads-air-soundink-rate" shouted Tempo in his Scouse accent. He saw some potential in us and offered to be our manager. With this, he would bring his experience of working on the Liverpool music scene, his contacts, and his vision of how we should be doing things from that point forward. We all agreed to have Tempo on board and looked forward to working with him over the coming months.

It was at this point that we were dealt another blow. Our drummer Luke announced that he was leaving the band. We were sad about this as he'd become a solid member of the crew, and with it being at such short notice leading up to our next set of gigs, we had to act fast to recruit another drummer. It was one of those moments again where we all had to try and think of anybody that we knew who could play drums. One of my mates came to mind; "I know who can drum" I said, "Aky", "Yeah, Aky can drum, let's see if he'll do it", said Tim. Aky aka 'James Ackroyd' was a mate of mine and Tims from school and we knew he was a good drummer. I got in touch with him and invited him over to our next rehearsal at The Legion. He agreed to join us as a temporary drummer and to help us out by playing at our next gig, which was going to be a big one.

We needed to get as much rehearsal time as we could, and due to us only having two nights per week at The Legion, we decided to practice at my house on weekends. I'd already had a music room set up in my back bedroom where we used to do some jamming and the odd 4-track recording, though I had never had a full drum kit in there. Aky set up his kit which took up a third of the room, then the rest of us crammed into the other side of the room. We started playing 'The Score', remember the song that got us kicked out of the Punch Bowl, we were loud, too loud, a full band playing a punk song at full volume in a terrace house with paper-thin internal walls meant only one thing.

As we got halfway through the song, my neighbour had already entered my house, no point in knocking; made her way upstairs and burst into the bedroom shouting "What the fuckin' hell do you think you're playing at!?". "You don't know the score" shouted Sam back at her. "I thought there'd been an explosion," she said. "Sorry about that", "We were just practising our songs" I replied. She calmed down after a few more expletives and told us to turn it down a bit. The thing is, you can only really go as low as the drum kit, which is loud anyway. We carried on, albeit a little bit lower in volume and we didn't hear from her again. The back bedroom sessions allowed us to get Aky up to speed and confident enough to play in the band and perform with us, but we knew at the same time, we still needed to recruit a permanent drummer and continued to spread the word.

CHARABANC TO LIVERPOOL

It was May 1998, and Tempo had arranged for us to perform at the prestigious Cavern Club in Liverpool after being in touch with one of his mates 'Alex McKechnie' who was the venue manager at the time. This was the real deal for us, as we'd all become big Beatles fans over the years of listening to their music, learning to play it, and then performing it. So, to be able to play at the venue that was the home of The Beatles would be an absolute honour and a privilege.

We had to go big with this, we couldn't just rock up to The Cavern as just the band, we needed an entourage to come along with us, and aptly booked a coach and spread the word. We went to see David Knights at the Keighley News to tell him all about it. He then had it all written up and published in the next week's newspaper, with follow-up mini articles each week until the weekend of the gig. We made a load of flyers and handed them out around the pubs, this was pre-Internet, so it was all physical stuff that you had to do to get the word out. We made some tickets and distributed them to a few of the local pubs to sell, The Fleece in Haworth and The

Druids Arms in Long Lee, we also had some to sell in the local indie music shop 'Mix Music' in Keighley which happened to be managed by our old drummer Simon Cartright. Things were getting very exciting; the hype was being built up and all we could do was hope we'd sell enough tickets to pay for the coach that we'd already booked and paid for in advance.

It was 8:30 am, the morning of the gig, and we all had to meet up on Hanover Street in Keighley to catch the coach. We all turned up with our gear, guitars, amps, and drum breakables, making sure we didn't forget anything as we did at the Queens Hall gig; now that would have been a catastrophe! We weren't the first to arrive though. There was a queue of people waiting, some familiar faces and some people we'd never met; new fans perhaps? this was brilliant. More people arrived, followed by the coach, which arrived promptly at 09:00 am. "ALL ABOARD", "The magical mystery tour is about to begin," shouted Ste.

During the ride out to Liverpool, we had our "2am" EP playing on the coach cassette player, plus a few Beatles albums to get the party started. Everyone was cracking open their tinnies that they'd brought along for the ride and singing along to the music, it was like the 'Jolly Boys Outing' episode from Only Fools and Horses.

By the time we got to Liverpool, most people were half-cut. The coach pulled into the Albert Docks car park around 11 am and we all terminated there. The driver told us that we all needed to be back by 7 pm on the dot, which wasn't such a bad curfew really, 8 hours of drinking was on the cards, though we did have to hold back a bit and be on our best behaviour as we had to perform at around 4 p.m. We got our gear off the coach and headed towards the City Centre.

After a longer than originally anticipated walk across Liverpool carrying our amps and speaker cabs, which got heavier with every step, my arms were like Mr Tickles! We eventually got to Mathew Street, and low and behold in front of us was the entrance to the world-famous Cavern Club. It was at the corner of the building which didn't look like much above ground, but as we winded our way down the spiral staircase to the bottom, we found ourselves in a red brick lined set of tunnels, the middle tunnel in particular was drawing our attention, and was the main one with the famous multicoloured wall as the backdrop to the stage that was set in front of it.

With it still being morning, the Club had only just opened, so there wasn't anyone there but us, which gave us a bit of time to look around the place and get used to our surroundings, taking it all in that we were not only in The Cavern Club for the first time in our lives, but we'd be playing here later that afternoon. Tempo introduced us to Alex. "Alright lads how are youz, I've been hearing lots about-yeh," said Alex. "All good mate", said Tim, "We're looking forward to playing here". "Well, I'm looking forward to havin-youz lads on, it's gonna be a great afternoon". Alex then showed us to the backstage room where we could leave our gear.

Our first impressions of The Cavern Club were overwhelming, it was like a temple for music with the stage as the altar and the coloured wall at the back as a shrine to the best in the business, it was immaculate. But backstage was quite the opposite, it was like what I can only describe as an outside toilet that had just been bombed. The walls were grubby with a mix of bad graffiti and mould, the toilet door was hanging off its hinges, with the toilet seat nicely placed down the side of the toilet bowl and covered in pee. But we'd seen worse, and so just cracked on with it.

As we were the last band on that afternoon, we got to soundcheck first, so without any hesitation, we were up on that stage, plugged in, tuned up, and away with it. It sounded mint and we couldn't wait to perform that afternoon. It was now time to see the sights and sounds of Liverpool and sample some of the beers of all the pubs on Mathew Street.

First up was The Cavern Pub, opposite the entrance to The Cavern Club. Here we found the place alive with The Beatles music on the jukebox and was in full swing with the tourists bopping about. We then zig-zagged our way down Mathew Street on a pub crawl, stopping at Lennon's Bar, which had a live duo playing more Beatles songs, and then on to **Abbey Road Bar,** which I believe is now called 'Flares', and yes, you've guessed it, more Beatles music. **After our 3rd pint** we headed to the second most famous bar on Mathew Street called Eric's, where many well-known punk bands played in the late 1970s and early 1980s (The Clash, Sex Pistols, Buzzcocks, and The Stranglers, to name but a few). This was followed by a few more traditional pubs, The King John and **The Grapes,** where we found our old friend 'Skoony' causing mischief again, but this time, he was stood up on top of a table in the middle of the pub whilst having a minor trouser dysfunction incident. At that point, we decided to leave and try out Flanagan's Irish bar and have a pint of Guinness while watching some old folks dance a jaunty jig. Last but no means least, we headed to the bottom of Mathew Street to the taproom of them all, The White Star which is where we'd find Bob Carlisle chatting with the natives in his Scouse tongue.

After a jolly afternoon on the beer, we needed to soak it all up before our performance at The Cavern and headed off for some food. I ended up in Burger King, which was my first experience of the franchise, I remember the burgers being a lot bigger than they are today. The rest of the band split across the city in search of other food places. We agreed to all meet back at The Cavern at 3:30 pm sharp. I headed back to The Cavern and rounded up as many of the entourage as I could. I was the first band member back; it was a lot busier than earlier in the day with one of the support bands already in full flow. I headed for the backstage room to get my bass guitar out of its case and made sure it was all still tuned up. The rest of the band started to arrive in dribs 'n' drabs until we were all back together.

The nerves started to kick in a bit as the clock neared 4 pm. I recall my jaw was starting to lock, I could hardly speak, the same was to be said about the rest of the band, which was more of a worry for Tim as he needed to sing. Although we'd played many gigs before without as much nervous tension between us, it's to be said that this must have been the most nervous we'd been, it's The Cavern Club after all, and we had to raise our game, no crappy performance, it had to be solid. The atmosphere outside was getting louder, it was buzzing with energy with everyone shouting for The Undecided, encouraging us to start the gig. We headed out.

The place was rammed! All I could see was a sea of heads from the front of the stage to the back of the main tunnel, and the same down each side tunnel. We all plugged in and readied ourselves. For the first song, yep, you've guessed it, 'The Score'. Sam and Ste started their guitar feedback, whilst I started the bass build-up, Aky then brought the drums in, all of us getting louder and louder in the build-up until I got to the end of the neck of my bass, basically the highest fret before you land on the pick-up, then BOOM.... into the first bar and then Tim comes in on vocals, "Who the hell is Sally, everybody knows she's a scally, well get out of here cos you don't know the score no more".

The whole place was bouncing, and I felt the nerves just ease off, my jaw relaxed, and it felt like I was surfing on the soundwaves that we were creating. The rest of the songs just flowed, and the tension soon disappeared, we were all on a high and finished the set with the following ditty in the style of "I Should Have Known Better" by The Beatles.

I……never knew what a twat Sam is

And I know that he stinks of piss

Yes, he does…. yes, he does, yes, he does………

And we all fucking hate yah

All right, now the lyrics are not exactly how Lennon & McCartney wrote it, and you might think this to be an insult to our lead guitarist, but it was more of a "we're not worthy" ode to Sam, and he bloody loved it! This became a regular song we'd sing out of respect, mainly at band rehearsals but also at the end of a gig, and there's no better place to sing this song than at The Cavern Club, the home of The Beatles.

Afterwards, we had crowds of tourists wanting our autographs, we were scribbling away on the backs of beermats, cigarette packets, and whatever else was waved in front of us. It was an absolute blast and pretty much sobered us all up. So, with that, we then went around all the same pubs again and celebrated until it was time to head back to the coach. Did we all get back in time for the 7 pm curfew? Did we fuck! And the coach driver was hell-bent on leaving without us all, but we managed to persuade him to hang back. It was going on 9 pm before we got everyone back on the coach and headed off back home.

It wasn't long before we got asked to play at The Cavern Club again, and over the next couple of years, we ended up playing there six times. Each time booking and then filling a coach. The second time we took Luke Parker's band Moondog (originally called Fire) to be our support, and we had two coach-loads of people joining us for more fun and shenanigans. It was on that occasion that Ste decided to wear around his neck, the grubby toilet seat from the backstage dressing room, he wore it for the whole gig before passing it around the crowd who then took turns wearing it around their necks and having a photo taken, it was like some kind of crazy ritual. Even my mum posed for a photograph taken with it on.

On a couple of our return trips, we ended up playing two gigs in a row, Friday night was at The Picket, Saturday afternoon we entertained at The Cavern again, and then another time playing The Cavern on Saturday and then at The Pogue Mahone on the Sunday. I do recall them being very long weekends for me as I had to drive to Liverpool then back home on the Friday, back to Liverpool on the coach for the Saturday gig, before returning home again. I must have been crazy!

The final time we played at The Cavern was in December 1999. When we arrived, we were told that the gig wasn't going to be held on the main stage in the main tunnel but was to be held on a different stage in another tunnel, one that we'd never been in before. The Cavern was bigger than we originally thought. The stage was bigger, and the tunnel was wider. We also noticed that the dressing room and toilets had been done up, all new paint, new carpet, new toilets, no graffiti, or mould, they were immaculate. The reason for this was that Sir Paul McCartney was in town and was to play at the Cavern with his band after we'd played there. So technically, we were the warmup act, albeit the day before.

So, as we left the stage after that gig, next up was Sir Paul*.

*The following day I watched Sir Paul McCartney on the Television playing live on the very stage that we were on the day before; he was joined by David Gilmour from Pink Floyd. It was a fantastic performance. I guess there'll be no more toilet seat wearing rituals happening again.

INITIATION TEST

It was the beginning of June 1998, and we were still celebrating our first successful gig at The Cavern Club, but at the same time, we knew we would be losing drummer number five. Aky was only a temporary drummer and left the band due to other commitments. The word for a new drummer was spouted about yet again but wasn't too long before Steve Smith (or Steve 80 as we used to call him*) came to audition with us at The Legion.

We started off with a few of our popular songs to ease Steve into our set and all was going well. "So, what do you reckon to our songs then Steve?" said Ste. "Erm, yeah I like some of them, and you've got some good upbeat tunes to play along to there". "I was just wondering, whilst performing if Tim could maybe move around a bit, give a bit more energy to the delivery". "Ha, ha. No mate, that's not my style" Replied Tim. So, we continued with a few more songs and thought nothing more of Steve's advice. But the fuse had already been lit. We stopped for a break. Steve sat down at a table in the middle of the room to relax and have a beer. Tim then went to get a pint from the bar, but as he walked across the room towards the door, he suddenly veered towards Steve and lamped him one square on the chin, and without breaking his stride, continued walking towards the door, and then exited the room.

WTF just happened!? Sam and I rushed over to Steve to see if he was alright. He was clutching his face and looked dazed.

"Did that just happen?", said Steve, "Not sure what happened there?" I replied. "I think it must be some kind of initiation test", said Sam. A few minutes later Tim entered the room with his pint, apologised to Steve, shook his hand and we all just cracked on with rehearsing as though nothing happened. Quite bizarre, but after that, Tim and Steve had a long chat and got on well, and he agreed to join the band as drummer number six.

We had a month of successful rehearsals with Steve, all except one time where Sam tripped over the cable that was plugged into my brand-new bass guitar. I'd just purchased an Epiphone Rivoli Bass, took it to our rehearsal at The Legion, tuned it all up and put it in my guitar stand before going to get a beer. We all headed for the bar, but Sam somehow managed to trip over my guitar lead which then pulled my bass over and snapped the headstock clean off. It was totally knackered, and I'd not even had the chance to play it. It was one of those head-in-your-hand moments. Sam did apologise, as it was an accident. I kept as cool as I could, though my brain was exploding inside! I did end up getting a free replacement the following week and I went on to perform with it for years to come. Following on from that slight hiccup, we booked a few back-to-back gigs, being at The Victoria Hotel in Keighley, The Snooty Fox in Oakworth and then back to Keighley to play at a place called 'Boothy's' which went down a treat. Steve's drumming was slick and sounded crisp, he owned probably the best drum kit that any of our drummers owned up to that point, and it showed.

Tempo had also noticed that we'd upped our game and were ready to record some of our songs in a proper music studio. He arranged the recording session at a studio in Liverpool called Hard City Records** which was run by a guy called 'Jim Turner'. It was a studio where several well-known Liverpool bands had recorded in the past. We needed a couple of our best songs and chose to record 'Feeling Better' which I had penned back in 1997 and a song that our new drummer Steve had written called 'Burning'.

When we arrived at the studio, we were greeted by a familiar face. It was Donald Ward. He was a friend of ours and a well-known musician from Haworth who played in many bands, one being The Whipping Post. He was a great trumpet player and provided the back-drop trumpet to our recording of 'Feeling Better'. Jim Turner also dropped some fantastic Harmonica onto the final recording of 'Burning'. After the recording session, we went to perform at The Picket that evening, before I ended up returning home and then boomeranging back the following day to perform at The Cavern Club as previously mentioned.

Once we received the final mastered recording, Tempo sent a copy of Feeling Better to be made into a dance remix by his mate Joe McKechnie, who was incidentally the brother of Alex from the Cavern. The house remix 'Feeling Even Better' was added to the single as a bonus track. We then needed to raise some capital to pay for the printing of the sleeves and pressing of the CD. I asked my boss Mike Bower who owned Link Telecom, a Telecommunications company in Keighley. He knew I was really into my music and wanted to help us out. He agreed to sponsor us and paid for the pressing of 500 singles on CD. Once we'd received the CDs, we distributed them around the local pubs and music shops, sold them at gigs and sent some off to a few major record labels too***. Other than a few CD's that we kept for ourselves, all copies found new homes and became our most popular release.

Not long after recording the single, Tempo arranged for us to create a video for the Feeling Better song and hired his mate Andy 'Easty' Eastwood to come to Haworth and film the band. We ended up filming all over the Bronte moorland, on the K&WVR Steam railway, down the cobbles of Main Street and then back at our hub, The British Legion. It was all done on a shoestring, and we enjoyed making it though it wasn't something we distributed and due to being pre-Internet, I doubt there are many copies of it left out there.

*The reason for calling him Steve 80 was due to him being a bit older than us and preferred 1980s music more than the 1990s music that we were all into at the time.

**The Hard City Records building was featured in the 2001 film 'The 51st State' (known as Formula 51 globally), which starred Samuel L Jackson and Robert Carlyle. Unfortunately, the building was demolished to make room for apartments in 2009. *Source: Reddit.com*

***We did receive some response letters back from Virgin Records, Columbia, Biglife and Revolver, though all said we didn't really fit in with what they were looking for at the time, and to try again in future, which we never did.

BETTER THAN BISCUITS

It was November 1998, and with the new single now on sale, we put a string of gigs together to promote it. We started locally at The Legion in Haworth, then on to a quirky little place called The Pop & Pasty Social Club in Keighley. From the outside it looked like a couple of terraced houses, but inside was a Phoenix Nights-esque type club with all the trimmings. We then branched out to Leeds*, then over to Hebden Bridge to debut at another prestigious venue on the music circuit being The Trades Club before ending the mini tour back at The Cavern Club in Liverpool.

The gig at The Trades Club led us to a little bit of a gem. We asked our mate Ian 'Scouse' Clarke if his band The Pipers would support us, and they agreed. With us having another Keighley band in support, they helped boost the touring crowd to travel over the hills to Hebden Bridge and helped raise our band profile with the club. Whilst we were there, Tempo made a good connection with the club manager, and he said he'd put the word out for us to be a support band for any signed bands that were playing at the club over the following months. It turned out that one of the bands to be playing there in the not-too-distant future were none other than Half Man Half Biscuit, who were luckily mates of Tempo's. He put in a good word, and we ended up with a support slot.

Half Man Half Biscuit are from Birkenhead and founded by Nigel Blackwell and Neil Crossley. They were known for their satirical post-punk album productions, such as 'Back in the DHSS', with songs like 'Fuckin' 'Ell it's Fred Titmus' and 'I Love You Because (you look like Jim Reeves)'. They were firm favourites of the late Radio1 DJ John Peel, who enjoyed having them play live sessions on his radio show in the early 1990s.

It was the afternoon of the gig, and we headed over the hills again and made our way to the Trade's Club. When we arrived, Tempo introduced us to Nigel, Neil, and the other members of Half Man Half Biscuit, before setting up our gear and running through the usual sound check routine. Once we were done, we headed out to sample some of the pubs of Hebden Bridge and chillax before the gig. After a few light ales, we headed back to the Trades Club. A huge queue had formed outside. We managed to get to the front after a bit of argy-bargy with some of the punters who thought we were jumping the queue, obviously not aware that we were the support band. The place was rammed. This is going to be a great gig, I thought to myself.

We plugged in and got ready. We were then introduced over the microphone as the support band "The Undecided from Keighley", to which we got maybe a handful of claps. To be honest, no one there had ever heard of us. As we got going, we could see the crowd gently start to nod and move about. Not knowing our songs, they weren't singing along, but you could see them starting to appreciate our music. One guy was standing right at the front, staring into Tim's face, he was moshing up and down and doing his best to put Tim off, and no; it wasn't Baz Houldsworth this time, it was a full-on Half Man Half Biscuit fan.

We then threw in our only cover song that we were performing at the time; it was a good one too, and one that must have been familiar to the Half Man Half Biscuit crowd as they all started singing along. It was a song called 'Capaldi's Café' originally by the band Deaf School, another Liverpool outfit that Tempo knew, and obviously, the crowd did too. We had the whole crowd going. At one point, the manager of Half

Man Half Biscuit collared Tempo and asked him if we could finish earlier than planned as we were too good and didn't want us to detract their fans. But we were having too much fun and continued our full set which ended with a huge cheer and applause, even the guy who was bothering Tim stopped and shook his hand saying we were brilliant.

We stayed to watch Half Man Half Biscuit perform, they were great and so were their fans. Afterwards, we were sat having a beer in the club bar, some of the fans were saying "Well done lads, you were great," and one fan even went on to say, "You were better than biscuits", which was a big positive for us and really nice to hear.

*See Fly Posting in Leeds story, page 124.

SIXTEEN DRUMMERS – THE STORY OF **THE UNDECIDED**

SIXTEEN DRUMMERS – THE STORY OF **THE UNDECIDED**

YOU SHUT UP SAM

In between promoting our new single at gigs, Tempo arranged for us to appear on the local radio station BCB in Bradford. When we arrived at the station, we were told to sit in a waiting area, *a kind of green room* until the DJ was ready to interview us. Sam had turned up with a pack of beer and was merrily drinking for a bit of Dutch courage before we went on air. He then started fidgeting about and without realising, his newly opened can of beer tipped over at the side of him and emptied into the sofa that he was sitting on. "Fuckin' 'Ell Sam, what are you doing," said Ste, "ah fuck, that's a full tinny gone," said Sam. "Sod the tinny" I replied, "look at the bloody mess you've made, and we've only been here 2 minutes". The sofa was soaked wet through, it looked like someone had taken a piss on it. "They're going to fuckin' kick us out of here before we get on the air at this rate," said Tempo.

Sam scurried to the toilets to get some paper towels, then tried his best to soak up the mess. We were then called into the studio. When we got in there, the DJ went through the gist of how the interview would go, where he'd play some of our songs in between and when we could play a song live on air. Unfortunately, it was at this point that I received an emergency call out from work and had to go sort something out, so missed out on being interviewed. The rest of the lads continued the show, and this is how things unfolded.

INT RADIO STUDIO, BCB RADIO, BRADFORD - EARLY AFTERNOON (12:30 pm) *

(Sam, Ste, Tim, Tempo, DJ, DJ Assistant)

Music fades in - playing a live acoustic version of "Feeling Better".

DJ:

"Excellent, yeah, and a bit of applause in the background, must have been doing something right."

"That's a version of Feeling Better, to which is one of three tracks on the CD, and I shall be playing the lead track a bit later on."

"Some quite interesting stuff you've got there, it says here, obviously a Keighley band, but you seem to have done a lot of the work in Liverpool."

Ste:

"That's right, we've been down and recorded a CD in Liverpool, done a few gigs down there – Cavern, Picket, Pogue Mahone, we've been down there quite a bit doing gigs. It's good!"

DJ:

"So, how's the scene down there…a bit different to being around Bradford and Keighley."

Tim:

"Just a bit livelier and a bit more going on really."

Sam:

"A better atmosphere."

Tim:

"Yeah, yeah."

Tempo:

"It's where it all began!"

DJ:

"Well, that's it, somewhere like The Cavern, you could definitely argue that anyway."

"I noticed when I was last around that neck of the woods, down Mathew Street in Liverpool, it does get extremely chocka."

"Full of a lot of underage drinkers last time I was over there."

Sam:

"A load of Japanese 'n' all."

DJ:

"One day you'll get a load of them waiting to take your photographs."

Tim:

"Yeah, we had him with a toilet seat around his neck last time, and at the end, up on-stage taking photographs of him."

Sam:

"With a toilet seat around their heads, taking it in turns, with a toilet seat."

DJ:

"And they just think ah, crazy English costume."

"Right, can you tell us something about this first track I'm going to play from the CD?"

Sam:

"It's the second track actually."

DJ:

"No, no, it's the first track."

Sam:

"It's changed?"

Ste:

"No, you shut up Sam."

Tim:

"Yeah, you keep quiet".

"We did it at Liverpool, like we said, took a day to do."

Ste:

"We did both tracks in that day."

Tempo:

"It's a love song."

Ste:

"It's called Burning anyway."

Sam:

"Set your life on fire!"

DJ:

"Er... yeah, here it is anyway."

INT Music plays – CD version of Burning.

DJ:

"That's Burning from The Undecided's CD, which is as far as I can tell, is just titled The Undecided. I'm sure the guys themselves will be able to tell us a little bit more about it and, more importantly, where to buy it from?"

Tim:

"Well, it's called the 'time is now', but that's just a working title, and is available at The Fleece in Haworth and The Druids Arms in Long Lee near Keighley."

DJ:

"Yes, I know The Fleece in Haworth very well, a fine drop of Timbo's in there."

Ste:

"Yeah, I'm the guitarist who lives there."

Tim:

"Not officially anyway."

DJ Assistant:

"I was in there yesterday, just at lunchtime."

DJ:

"Really!"

Tempo:

"That's what it's done to him, look."

DJ:

"That's the problem with anything like that, technically not supposed to mention product placement on the air."

DJ Assistant:

"Other pubs are available."

Tim:

"Ha, ha, yeah, and they've all got nice booze."

DJ:

"Right then, you've got one more track for us anyway, can you tell us something about the track you're going to play?"

Tim:

"We're going to do an Acoustic, it's called 'Absolute Madness', it was written by Steven, so he could shed some light on it."

Tempo:

"It's all about the chaos Stevie, all that goes on within the band."

Ste:

"It's absolute madness."

DJ:

"And no sight of Pork Pie hats or two-tone clothing?"

Tim:

"Oh, no, no"

Tempo:

"Even though we do like that."

Tim:

"Oh yeah, we do like' em but, we can't play any wind instruments."

DJ:

"Aye, let's have a listen."

Ste:

"Anyway, when you've snapped out of your daydream Sam."

Sam:

"I've been told to keep my gob shut, so I am doing."

Tempo:

"You can still play though!"

INT – The Undecided plays a live acoustic version of Absolute Madness.

DJ:

"Absolute Madness there from The Undecided."

"So, before you go, we'll be leaving off with another track of yours from the CD."

"When are you next likely to be about, doing the live gigs?"

Tim:

Well, we've got one up at the Haworth British Legion on Boxing Day, oh, and one on New Year's Eve as well, but we're sort of in limbo with drummers at the moment."

Tempo:

"We're auditioning for a new drummer."

DJ:

"It's the eternal Spinal Tap problem then?"

Tim:

"Yeah, we're looking for drummer number seven."

"If anyone wants to have a bit of a try out, they can ring us, any time through the day, for an audition."

DJ:

"A chance at fame folks"

"What are you going to be leaving us with, something

atypical of what you've been playing."

"Now this track that you played for us first, 'Feeling Better', this is the dance mix, which I shall be playing part of from the CD, can you explain how you came to record a dance mix of it?"

Tim:

"Yeah, a friend of the band is a DJ in Liverpool at Crash FM, so, he's made it, and he goes out by the name DJ Tempo, he goes around clubs and, he's done it for us, which is a nice change, a different style of music to our own."

DJ Assistant:

"Credited as Stardust on the inner sleeve, I noticed."

DJ:

"Ha, Ha, yeah that's how it is in Liverpool, all these different names, you've got to keep the social off your back like."

"Any listeners in Liverpool by the way, I'm sorry, but you're living in Liverpool, and we're allowed to tell scouse jokes."

DJ Assistant:

"Why are they like Batman? ...They can't go out without Robin, ha, ha, there you go."

DJ:

"Let's hear some of this dance mix then and thank you to The Undecided."

Tim/Ste/Sam/Tempo:

"Thank you, thanks a lot, bye, Merry Xmas."

INT Music plays – CD version of Feeling Even Better (dance mix).

END

*The audio recording of the BCB radio interview can be heard at the following link:

https://soundcloud.com/user-191071063/bcb-radio-interview-absolute-madness-live

FLY POSTING IN LEEDS

Among the many gigs we played in Liverpool, we also had a run of gigs in Leeds. Tempo lived over that way back then and had arranged for us to play at a few venues around the city. To promote the gigs, we decided to create some large A2 size posters and paste them up wherever we could. Ste turned up in his Nissan Bluebird with a bucket of ready-mixed wallpaper paste, a brush, and a boot full of rolled-up posters that we had printed.

"Right, I'll start over here, this looks like a good spot as other people have posted some posters here", said Ste. He then got to work and started to slop up his first poster over an existing poster on a bus shelter. "Woah, woah Stevie" shouted Tempo, "You can't just paste over someone else's poster mate". "Why" replied Ste. "There's an etiquette to flyposting, you don't post over someone else's posters unless it's dated in the past" exclaimed Tempo, "Otherwise we may end up in a bit of a street battle with the other promoters". Ste soon got the picture and plied the remaining posters to the spaces in between the other band's posters on the various bus stops, billboards, and derelict shop windows.

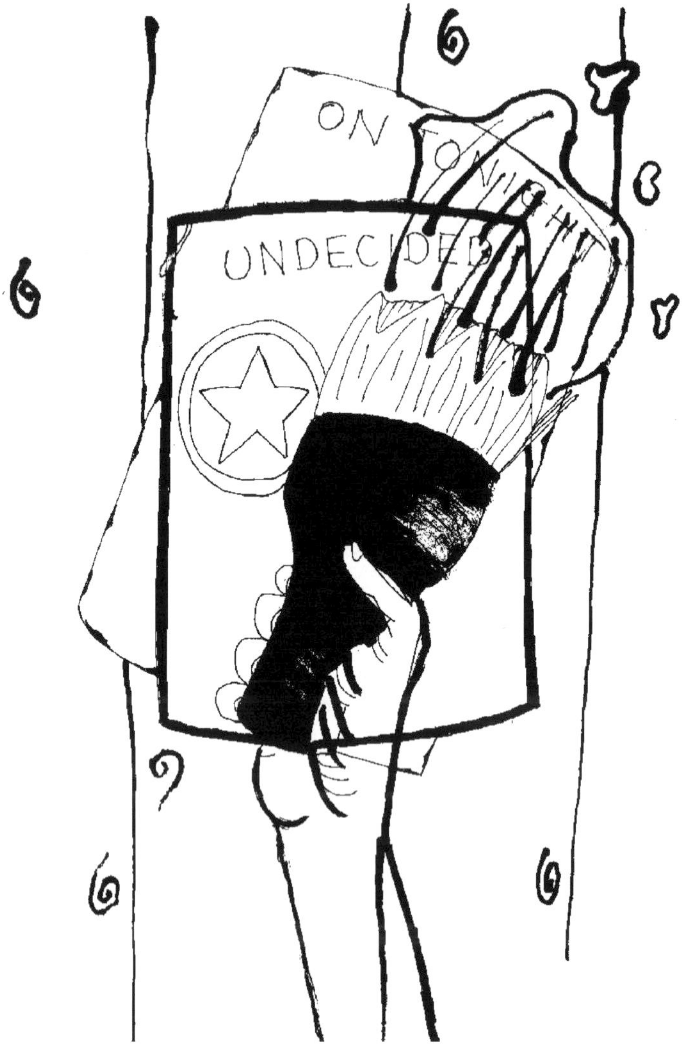
ON
UNDECIDED

After decorating half of Leeds, Tempo and Ste returned to Keighley and had a few beers to celebrate their achievements in the Volunteers pub known as the 'Volts', before meeting up with the rest of us to discuss the upcoming Leeds gigs and what money we should expect to make. This is how things unfolded.

First up was The Fenton, which was a bar up near the University of Leeds on Woodhouse Road. We played in the upstairs room along with a few punk bands that were on tour. Some of our punky songs were appreciated by the Mohican-donning crowd, though most of our set was indie rock, which was lost on them, well you can't win them all. We shared the door fee with the other bands, though this amounted to no more than a few beers, so we left in the hope that our next gig would make up for it.

The next gig was at Royal Park which is located next door to the Brudenell Social Club in the Headingley area of Leeds. This was a firm favourite with all the students and was quite busy, though we ended up playing down in the cellar bar and seemed to be competing for an audience with a band that was playing upstairs at the same time as us. We ended up with a pittance of the door fee, maybe only enough to cover the fuel costs. We were now in need of a big money earner at our next gig.

Finally, there was The Golden Eagle. Now this place was one to remember, but not for the right reasons. We got there and found ourselves in a quiet pub. It was so quiet, that there was only us and the barman in the building. We set up our gear opposite the bar in a semi-circular-shaped room. The barman started telling us that "The shape of the room lent towards it having the best acoustics in Leeds", in a very genuine tone of voice, though we took this as complete and utter nonsense, ordered a beer then sat and waited for people to arrive.

An hour passed by and still no one. It was just us and Billy Bullshit. I went over to the main entrance and popped my head out, looked left, then right, and noticed the whole street was empty, no cars, no people, no noise, it was a ghost town. It got to about 9:00 pm and not a sausage, so we plugged in and started the gig, playing only to the barman, Tempo, and a couple of people that we'd brought with us. We played the whole set and not one local punter entered the building. What a complete and utter dive it was, and a total waste of our time. We didn't get paid as we were told we'd receive what was taken on the door, which was sod all.

With the band finances now dwindling and the poor run of gigs we were having, things were starting to strain in the band. Arguments had started and we were all getting a bit pissed off about not earning any money from gigs. To top things off, Steve had already announced that he was going to be leaving the band after the run of gigs in Leeds to concentrate more on his business, which left us drummerless for the sixth time, and just before Christmas when we had already booked our usual festive gig at The Legion. It wasn't the best of times.

SIXTEEN DRUMMERS – THE STORY OF **THE UNDECIDED**

PHOTO GALLERY

SIXTEEN DRUMMERS – THE STORY OF **THE UNDECIDED**

Just before band practice - The British Legion 1997

The Limo, Main Street, Haworth - 1997

SIXTEEN DRUMMERS – THE STORY OF **THE UNDECIDED**

Performing at The White Bear, Eastburn – 1997

Ste, Sam and Tim with the mighty Nissan Bluebird - 1997

SIXTEEN DRUMMERS – THE STORY OF **THE UNDECIDED**

Our first gig at The Cavern Club - 1998

Lugging gear, Mathew Street, Liverpool – 1998

SIXTEEN DRUMMERS – THE STORY OF **THE UNDECIDED**

Ste and Dean, backstage at The Cavern Club - 1998

The Undecided set in stone – Haworth Moor - 1998

SIXTEEN DRUMMERS – THE STORY OF **THE UNDECIDED**

Tempo and Crew, Keighley - 1998

Did Smartphones really exist back in 1998?

SIXTEEN DRUMMERS – THE STORY OF **THE UNDECIDED**

Our 2nd gig at The Cavern Club - 1998

My mum, The Cavern Club - 1998

SIXTEEN DRUMMERS – THE STORY OF **THE UNDECIDED**

At the Picket, Liverpool - 1998

The Pop & Pasty Social Club, Keighley - 1998

SIXTEEN DRUMMERS – THE STORY OF **THE UNDECIDED**

Some of our entourage - 1998

SIXTEEN DRUMMERS – THE STORY OF **THE UNDECIDED**

A few of our drummers, Luke Matthews, Lionel Skerratt, James Ackroyd, Carl Stipetic, Gary Dwyer (with cameraman 'Easty'), Luke Parker

SIXTEEN DRUMMERS – THE STORY OF **THE UNDECIDED**

Photoshoot – Harden Moor – 1999

Group Photo, Guide Fest - 2004

SIXTEEN DRUMMERS – THE STORY OF **THE UNDECIDED**

With drummer number 10, Daniel Green, Haworth - 2002

At the Parkside Club, Haworth before drinking the place dry - 2002

SIXTEEN DRUMMERS – THE STORY OF **THE UNDECIDED**

Tim & Koe - IVOLV Studio, Idle, Bradford - 2010

Julie - IVOLV Studio, Idle, Bradford - 2010

Rocking away with my son Lewie on Tambourine, The Aire Do - 2010

The last band practice, Haworth Community Centre - 2011

SIXTEEN DRUMMERS – THE STORY OF **THE UNDECIDED**

30 years on - Tim, Ste, Koe – Long Lee, Keighley - 2024

More photos can be found on our Facebook page at:

https://www.facebook.com/undecidedrockers

DAGGY'S DIARY

Over the years, we gained many fans who became part of our entourage attending the many gigs we played, and one person in particular who attended more than any other was Mark "Daggy" Tempest. He is a true music fan, and especially of live music. He's been to hundreds of gigs over the years starting way back in the 1970s when the punk scene made its stamp on society and became a whole new music genre. He became a big fan of punk and attended many early performances from The Sex Pistols, The Clash, Buzzcocks, The Damned and many more. He also kept a record of all the gigs he'd attended, with band names, support acts, and venues, and he also added a score out of 5 for the band's performance. 1 star is poor, and up to 5 stars is excellent. Daggy has kindly allowed me to show some of the diary in the following photos where he attended The Undecided gigs and scored our performances. As you can see, we didn't always make the grade, but on one or two performances we did stand out.

SIXTEEN DRUMMERS – THE STORY OF **THE UNDECIDED**

22/11/95 -
235. FRANK SIDEBOTTOM ***** - FEAST AND FIRKIN LEEDS
236. 1996 - THE UNDECIDED *½ - SHOULDER OF MUTTON KEIGHLEY
237. 1996 - THE UNDECIDED *½ - SHOULDER OF MUTTON KEIGHLEY
238. 30/11/96 - THE UNDECIDED * - CON CLUB WILSDEN
239. 1/2/97 - THE UNDECIDED ** - DRUIDS KEIGHLEY
240. 4/4/97 - THE UNDECIDED ** - DRUIDS KEIGHLEY
241. 23/5/97 - THE UNDECIDED **½ - KINGS HEAD KEIGHLEY
242. 30/5/97 - THE UNDECIDED ***½ - WHITE BEAR EASTBURN
243. 12/9/97 - THE UNDECIDED **½ - DRUIDS KEIGHLEY
244. 26/9/97 - THE UNDECIDED **½ - WHITE BEAR EASTBURN
245. 3/10/97 - THE UNDECIDED ** - VICTORIA HOTEL KEIGHLEY
246. 7/10/97 - ECHO AND THE BUNNYMEN ***½ - TOWN & COUNTRY CLUB LEEDS
247. 11/10/97 - THE UNDECIDED ***½ - ROBBOS KEIGHLEY
248. 19/12/97 - CAST ****½ - BRADFORD ST GEORGES HALL
249. 26/12/97 - THE UNDECIDED ***½ - ROBBOS KEIGHLEY
250. 10/1/98 - THE UNDECIDED **½ - THREE HORSES KEIGHLEY
251. 15/5/98 - THE UNDECIDED **½ - THE FENTON LEEDS
252. 22/5/98 - THE UNDECIDED **½ - WHITE BEAR EASTBURN
253. 23/5/98 - THE UNDECIDED *** - BRITISH LEGION HAWORTH
254. 10/6/98 - HEAVY PLANT CROSSING * - THE UNDECIDED *½ - VICTORIA HOTEL KEIGHLEY

SIXTEEN DRUMMERS – THE STORY OF **THE UNDECIDED**

```
255. 11/8/98  THE UNDECIDED ***  - SNOOTY FOX OAKWORTH
256. 22/8/98  THE UNDECIDED ***  - BOOTHS KEIGHLEY
257. 29/8/98  THE UNDECIDED **** - CAVERN LIVERPOOL
258. 4/9/98   THE UNDECIDED ***  - BRITISH LEGION HAWORTH
259. 6/9/98   THE PIPERS *       - GAS CLUB KEIGHLEY
260. 11/9/98  THE UNDECIDED **   - HARROGATE ARMS HARROGATE
261. 24/9/98  THE UNDECIDED ***  - GLOBE KEIGHLEY
262. 25/9/98  THE UNDECIDED ***  - POP N PASTY KEIGHLEY
263. 29/10/98 THE UNDECIDED ***  - DAVIDS KEIGHLEY
264. 7/11/98  THE UNDECIDED ***  - BRITISH LEGION HAWORTH
265. 13/11/98 ASPIRE ** - THE UNDECIDED *** POP AND PASTY KEIGHLEY
266. 14/11/98 THE UNDECIDED ***  - ROYAL PARK LEEDS
267. 28/11/98 THE UNDECIDED ***½ - CAVERN LIVERPOOL
268. 26/12/98 THE UNDECIDED ***  - HAWORTH BRITISH LEGION
269. 30/1/99  THE UNDECIDED **½  - THE CRAVEN SKIPTON
270. 12/1/99  THE UNDECIDED **** - HEBDEN BRIDGE TRADES CLUB
     " "  "   HALF MAN HALF BISCUIT - **½ -  "   "
271. 27/2/99  THE UNDECIDED ***  - CAVERN LIVERPOOL
272. 27/3/99  THE UNDECIDED ***  - BRITISH LEGION HAWORTH
273. 16/4/99  THE UNDECIDED ***  - V.C HOTEL KEIGHLEY
```

SIXTEEN DRUMMERS – THE STORY OF **THE UNDECIDED**

274, 31/7/99 · THE UNDECIDED · ✱✱✱½ - CHEESE + TRUMPET KEIGHLEY.
275, 30/10/99 THE UNDECIDED - ✱✱✱ · CHEESE + TRUMPET KEIGHLEY.
276, 10/8/03 THE UNDECIDED - ✱✱ - THE GUIDE KEIGHLEY
277 29/6/04 - JERRY LEE LEWIS ✱✱✱ - CHUCK BERRY ✱✱✱✱ TOWN AND COUNTRY CLUB - BRADFORD
278 17/3/05 · BREED - ✱✱✱ - THE VIBRATORS · ✱✱✱✱ AIREVALLEY GAS CLUB - KEIGHLEY
279, 6/5/06 - FRANK SIDEBOTTOM ✱✱✱✱ ROCK + HIEFER THORNTON
280, 27/7/06 · THE SEX PISTOLS EXPERIENCE ✱✱✱✱ · GAS CLUB KEIGHLEY
281 ? /07 - THE SEX PISTOLS EXPERIENCE ✱✱✱✱ GAS WORKS BRADFORD
282 ? /07 - REBEL TRUCE · SEX PISTOLS EXPERIENCE · RIOS LEEDS
283, 20/12/07 - THE SEX PISTOLS EXPERIENCE - ✱✱✱✱ - GAS CLUB KEIGHLEY
284 /07 - THE GET GUNS ✱✱✱ ½ - GAS CLUB KLY.
285 18/4/09 - REBEL TRUCE · ✱✱✱✱ GAS CLUB KTY
286 15/11/09 · THE UNDECIDED - ✱✱✱✱ - HAWORTH LEGION
288, 8/5/09 - REBEL TRUCE - GAS CLUB - ✱✱✱✱
289, - /09 - THE UNDECIDED - PRVIAS - ✱✱✱✱
290, 21/11/09 - THE UNDECIDED - KLY CRICKET CLUB - ✱✱✱✱
291, 17/7/10 - THE UNDECIDED · ✱✱✱ ½ · CLIFFE CASTLE
292, 29/8/10 - THE UNDECIDED · ✱✱✱✱ - WAGON LANE BINGLEY
293, 3/9/10 - THE BUZZCOCKS - MYRTEL PARK BINGLEY - ✱✱✱
294, 6/2/11 · DEAF SCHOOL · ✱✱✱✱ - NEW ROSCOE - LEEDS

SIXTEEN DRUMMERS – THE STORY OF **THE UNDECIDED**

295, 15/10/11 - THE UNDICIDED - ~~****~~ - BRITISH LEGION HAWORTH
296, 29/12/12 - THE SEX PISTOLS EXPIERENCE ~~*****~~ - EXCHANGE ARTS CENTRE KLY
297 APRIL 2014 - IDIANIC - ~~***~~ - CRICKETERS KEIGHLEY
298, 22/11/14 - DEAF SCHOOL - ~~*****~~ - TRADES CLUB HEBDEN BRIDGE
299, 5/9/15 - DEAF SCHOOL - ~~*****~~ 2 - BINGLEY FESTIVAL.
300,
301, 20/5/16 ROXY MUSIQUE - ~~****~~ 12 EXCHANGE CLUB KLY
302 18/11/16 - THE STONES - ~~****~~ 12 EXCHANGE CLUB KLY
303, 27/12/18 - THE SEX PISTOLS EXPIERENCE - ~~*****~~ EXCHANGE KLY

Daggy - 1998

CHAPTER 4

ON A ROLL

BROTHERLY LOVE

Christmas was looming, we had our usual big-payer gig booked at the Legion and with the lack of a drummer, we weren't sure if we could do it. But with a stroke of luck and in the nick of time, we received some positive news. We'd managed to find drummer number seven, Lionel Skerratt, a young lad from Bingley. He was a good fit for the band and settled in after a couple of rehearsals. We had our Xmas time gig at the British Legion in Haworth and had a great evening, all went to plan with no cock ups, Lionel played well, and we had a merry time of it taking a few hundred quid on the door. With the new single still selling well, we managed to end 1998 on a high and looked forward to a new year.

We rolled into 1999, and I guess we were going to party like it was. We booked several new gigs. First up was The Craven pub in Skipton. It was a new venue as we'd not ventured to Skipton with the band. Again, it was the usual routine, get all the gear into the building, set it all up and chillax before the gig. But we arrived earlier than usual so we could have a few beers around the town, and go on a bit of a pub crawl, which was helped by the fact that the landlord of The Craven pub was a great guy and had allowed us to leave our gear there overnight so we could have a few drinks.

We headed off into the town and it wasn't too long before we ended up getting split up, Sam and Tempo went off together leaving me, Tim, Ste and Lionel to go on a pub crawl and sample a few real ales. We all managed to meet up again a few hours later. "Ayup Sam, Tempo, where did you get to?" said Ste. "We've just been around a few pubs," said Tempo. "He's been chatted up" said Sam, "yeah I think we may have been in a gay bar without realising it" said Tempo, "Gay bar" replied Tim, "I didn't know there were gay bars in Skipton", "Must have been, we were there for ages, and he was getting chatted up," said Sam. This conversation continued and rolled on into an argument. It was obvious that everyone was starting to get a bit too merry. We all headed back to the Craven pub.

When we got there, some of our mates had arrived including Dean and Heather. We'd lost track of time and had to plug in and play immediately. But as things panned out, it became obvious that we'd had one too many on our pub crawl, we were loud, out of sync, slurring and wobbling about the place during our first set. Tempo kept hiding behind this pillar at the back of the room, then popping his head out and pulling faces at us, he was properly hammered, and I was trying my best not to lose it or burst into hysterical laughter as I fought with my bass to keep a tune going. After a few glasses of water to sober us up, we returned to a more sensible order and improved our performance on the second set.

After the gig, we headed off towards a nightclub called After Dark, and then all hell broke out. We were all walking down this back street when suddenly Tim and his brother Dean started arguing and then ended up brawling with each other. Fists were flying, shirts were being ripped, and then they ended up on the floor scuffling about. Me and Ste grabbed Tim while Heather and Sam grabbed Dean to pull them apart, we were all wrestling and shouting at them to stop fighting, it was like trying to calm down Phil and Grant Mitchel from Eastenders. After a long battle, and plenty of arguing, things eventually calmed down, and we continued with our evening of drunkenness.

SIXTEEN DRUMMERS – THE STORY OF **THE UNDECIDED**

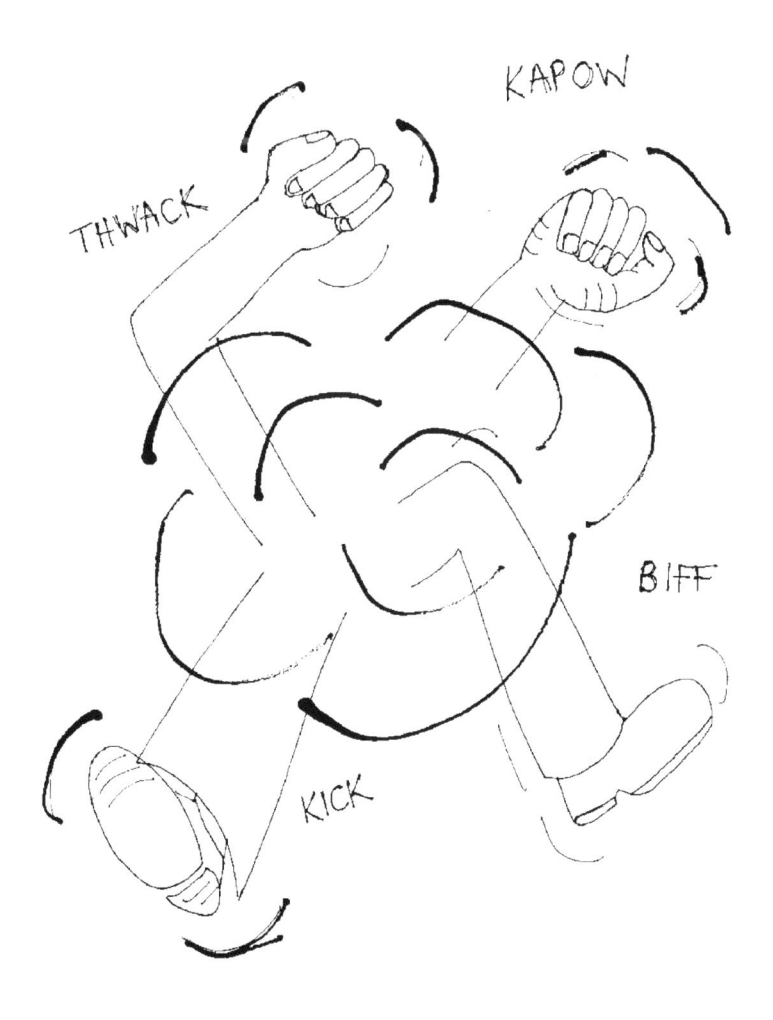

The next few gigs were less beer-fuelled, we had another at The British Legion in Haworth, one at the Druids Arms in Long Lee, another trip out to The Cavern in Liverpool, and then at a local festival, 'The Keighley Festival', which took place at The Victoria Hall in Keighley. It was a mini-festival showcasing some local bands arranged by Johnny Friendly aka 'John Gow' who appeared in bands such as The Big Bang and Johnny and the Poorboys.

The Keighley festival played out over four days, and we performed again with Moondog in support, whilst the other days saw the bands Kinesis, 3 Men and a Bass, Aspire, Hollow Horse, The Big Bang and Eponymous showcase their music. The festival was well received and sparked off several other music events at Victoria Hall over the following years.

A BENEFIT FOR KOSOVO

It was June 1999, and the Kosovo War had just ended. It was all over the TV and the UK Government was putting together some relief packages to help the many displaced Kosovans. This ended up getting into the consciousness of a group of people who arranged for a benefit gig for Kosovo which was to be held at The Duchess on Vicar Lane in Leeds. Tempo ended up being called by the organisers and asked if we'd like to take part and perform at the benefit gig, to which we agreed.

We'd never played at The Duchess before, though were very aware of it being quite a well-renowned venue, with a rich history of hosting iconic bands and musicians, such as Nirvana, Oasis, Blur, Manic Street Preachers, The Verve and many more. We were the first band to arrive. We loaded our gear in and started setting up, then I noticed a familiar face at the bar. It was one of my mates, Tony Leighton*. He'd seen one of the posters that had been put up, probably on one of the bus shelters, and came to give us some support.

Eventually, the other bands arrived, being Resin, Euphony

and Insense**. We were up on stage first and at that point, with it being early on, we only had a small audience, being the promoters, Tony, and the members of the other bands; oh, and the barman too. Well, it would have to do, as we were on a timer.

We plugged in, we played, we rocked, and we did our bit. Afterwards, we stayed on to watch the other bands and it started to get quite busy. It was obvious that these were all Leeds-based bands, and so had their own crowd turn up when they were performing, but that's how it can be with some of these gigs, it's swings and roundabouts, although it was a little more comforting than playing at The Golden Eagle the year before, and we did raise quite a bit of money too for the Kosovo appeal.

*If you've ever wondered why I am called Koe (pronounced Koo), then look no further than Tony Leighton, he came up with the nickname back in 1989, comparing me to the Dutch international footballer Ronald Koeman. The name has stuck ever since. Tony now runs 'Open Decks' which started at Hyde Park Book Club in Leeds. I DJ'd there a few times over the years and is now held monthly at Amity Brew Co in Farsley.

**There had become a rumour that we'd been playing alongside Coldplay at this gig, but it turned out it was the band Insense, who later changed their name to The Music, and ended up with record deals with Capitol, Virgin and Polydor and released a top 10 album. Their lead singer Robert Harvey is now a touring musician with the band Kasabian. Incidentally, Coldplay did play at The Duchess only two weeks after us, which may have been the cause for confusion.

PARTY AT THE MANOR

Sam had been asked by this bloke at The British Legion if our band could play at a private party in his house. I think he was a committee member, and he lived in the nearby village of Denholme. The chap offered to pay us handsomely, so it was a no-brainer, and we were all up for it. I remember us all talking about this at our next band rehearsal, we were all imagining playing in someone's front living room, how crazy that would be, all squashed in, blasting out our music from the back of the sofa, while this guy's family and friends would be all crammed in at the other side of the room. But this wasn't the case.

When we arrived at the address we'd been given, it wasn't the small, terraced house we'd all been thinking about. Stood in front of us was this big manor house, set back from the road within its own grounds with well stocked gardens. On the big open lawn at the front of the manor was a 9-hole putting green and was in full swing, with people cracking balls everywhere whilst running around with their tinnies in their hands. Just beyond a row of rhododendrons, must be posh,

SIXTEEN DRUMMERS – THE STORY OF **THE UNDECIDED**

you could just make out the top of a big marquee at the side of the house and the party was already rocking away.

We approached the marquee and were greeted by the hosts, "Welcome, welcome all, thanks for coming, make yourselves at home, there's a free bar on, so get stuck in and enjoy". "I feel a session coming on," said Sam, "Oh yes, this is gonna be a gooden" I replied. I wanted to let my hair down at this gig as it was one of those rare occasions where I didn't have to drive the van and cart all the gear around, I just turned up with my Bass guitar as the PA and amps were all laid on by the host.

We all got stuck into the free beer and had a wander around the grounds to take in all the fun and games and admire the spectacle. After a few hours of alfresco drinking, we decided to have a go at the putting green. We were pretty much blotted by this time and ended up whacking balls all over creation. This continued until it was time to play the gig, which couldn't come too soon, otherwise we'd be in no fit state to play.

We got the call to play, and all the partygoers had assembled in front of the stage area. It was twilight, and the party lights and garden lanterns all came on, it was a great atmosphere. Although we were half-cut, we were playing well, though I was in a bad state of needing the toilet. I'd not had the chance to go for a pee before our performance, and it all built up, I was doing my best to ignore it, but it was killing me, I was playing my bass, all crossed legged, wiggling about on the spot, I must have looked like Little Richard dancing. As soon as we'd finished, I threw my bass off to one side and dived into the bushes to water the plants.

I've never felt relief like it!

It was another successful gig, and we'd certainly entertained the crowd, though later in the evening some trouble had started between a few partygoers, *a bit too much gin if you ask me*, people were arguing, and accusations were flying about the place. We all ended up being told to leave and go home which was a bit of a blow, though we certainly did enjoy ourselves up to that point.

RAVING BONKERS!

Here's a little story to end our run of gigs in 1999. We were invited to play again at the Victoria Hall in Keighley, though this wasn't the usual kind of event that we'd been playing at over the years with bands and musicians. This event was to be a dance music event called 'Vinyl Dreamz', a kind of rave, which boasted that it was the start of something big and had a host of DJs playing, including Rachel Auburn of the Tidy Girls, M-Zone, Andy Pendle and Lewis T to name but a few. They also had a large 20K music system, light show, and dancers. So, where the hell did we fit in?

Although I am quite into my dance music, in fact, I probably listen to it more than rock music and love a bit of Techno, House and Drum & Bass, but the rest of the band weren't interested in that kind of music. So, it took a bit of convincing to get them to play at this venue. I mentioned we'd be paid quite a bit for it and needed to get some money in the kitty, and with that, all got on board.

When we arrived, we ended up with a large stage to ourselves in the big hall which was all darkened off but had flashing lights and lasers beaming about all over the place. There was this huge set of speakers at either side of the stage, like the ones you get at large outdoor festivals. We saw loads of young girls dressed in hardly anything, or should I say Scantily Clad, roller skating all around the place and handing out sweets to the crowd of ravers that were gathered in front of us. The ravers had come from all around, probably not knowing what kind of music we would be playing. But we soon gave it to them, and fuck me, did we sound loud, it was booming out of those bass bins. We blasted through our set, sticking to our most up-tempo songs and no slow numbers or acoustic songs. Everyone seemed to enjoy the show, even though we were kind of out of place, with one band and 20 DJs, we must have been raving bonkers!

SIXTEEN DRUMMERS – THE STORY OF **THE UNDECIDED**

MY GUITAR'S TURNED TO JELLY

As we headed into the year 2000 and everyone was worrying whether their computers would stop working and the world would end in an apocalypse, we were more worried that for all the gigs we'd done and been paid for, we had very little to show for it. Most of our income ended up in management costs and we were getting quite frustrated with this as we needed new equipment and wanted to record a new album; something had to give. Unfortunately, this was to be our manager Tempo, and I had drawn the short straw of giving him the bad news.

I met him in the Town Hall square in Keighley and delivered the blow. He was not happy with this as he'd put a lot of time and effort into getting us gigs, raising our band profile, and getting us connected with his mates in Liverpool, which I told him we'd very much appreciated. After a lot of effing and jeffing, we went our separate ways and that was the last time we had any contact with him for a good while into the future.*

Following on from Tempo's departure we regrouped and started to plan some paid gigs to allow us to build up a fund to record an album. As the money started coming in, we searched for local recording studios and came across the 'In A City' studio in Bradford. The place was run by a guy called Carl Stipetic**, whom I can only describe as a nice guy, absolutely bonkers, and a musical genius. We rocked up to the studio situated in Carlisle Business Centre in the Manningham area of Bradford. His studio was kitted out well with old-school tech compared to today's digital recording studios, he had this huge Soundcraft Ghost mixing desk and a big 24-track reel-to-reel recorder, that he kept whizzing back and forth between takes.

During our first recording session, Sam wasn't his usual self, he'd not brought any beer with him though he seemed a bit all over the place and acting odd. After quizzing him we discovered that he'd been spiked with some magic mushrooms before coming to the studio and was now hallucinating. When he was in the recording booth doing his takes on the lead guitar you could hear him giggling and then shouting down the microphone, "My guitars turned to jelly, it's all flopping about in my hands", we were all laughing our heads off. We decided to leave the lead guitar parts for another day.

After several months of toing and froing from the studio, we ended up with an album worth of songs recorded, which included 'Come Rain or Shine', 'Why You', 'All Yours', 'Absolute Madness', 'Not So Plain Jayne', 'Pot of Gold', 'The Girl', '4-Track Dream', 'Talkin 'bout The Future', 'Life's What

You Make It' and 'Instrumental Mental'. The album title was 'Like a Dove', named after one of our earlier songs. We walked away with a DAT tape of the recordings and a master CD copy and decided to run some copies and create the sleeves ourselves. Dean Baldwin designed the cover, a collage of different images and some photos of us dotted about in between and had a photonegative effect over the top. The inner sleeve had a photograph of us playing at The Cavern Club. I don't think we sold as many copies as we did with our single, only maybe a few hundred, before we released it to the Internet, which was in its infancy back then, with no Facebook, Instagram or TikTok. We had Myspace! I remember trying to upload all the songs via a 56K dial-up modem, it took bloody ages. How times have changed!

*The next time Ste and I bumped into Tempo was June 2009. We found him working at an Oasis gig at Heaton Park in Manchester. We made up and put all our differences in the past, water under the bridge so to speak, and he even went out of his way to sneak us into the VIP area.

**Carl ended up being drummer number eight and helped us complete the final few songs on the album, this was due to Lionel having to leave partway through to head off to university, before pursuing a career at Warp Records, the music label of some of my favourite musical artists such as Aphex Twin, Autechre, and Boards of Canada. What a lucky lad!

HOSPITALITY

It was summer 2000 and we'd been invited to go see Oasis perform at the Reebok Stadium in Bolton. The invite came from our good friend Jason Rhodes who was Noel Gallagher's guitar technician and roadie. We all knew Jason who was from Keighley and was connected to the local music scene, he also happened to be related to my cousin. Jason had put the tickets aside for us at the box office at the stadium, and all we needed to do was turn up.

We all met at Rossi's café in Keighley to have breakfast before the journey. After bacon butties and a brew, we made our way to the train station, stopping off at the bookies for a quick bet, then at the newsagents for the daily paper en route. It was routine to do that back then. When we got to the train station, we'd just missed our train to Leeds. "No worries," said Ste, "There's another one in 10 minutes. "But we must catch that one, so we don't miss the connecting train to Bolton," I said. As we were hanging around for the train, Ste noticed this business card printing machine installed in the ticket office and decided to get some cards printed for the band to hand out at gigs. The thing is it wasn't the quickest machine at printing. The next train arrived a few minutes later, "Hurry up Ste FFS, the trains here" I shouted. "Hold on, it's nearly done" replied Ste. The rest of us got on the train and stood in the doorway asking the guard to hold on a minute, then you could see Ste running down the ramp towards the platform, waving his new cards and shouting "Got 'em, hold the doors". He jumped onto the train just in the nick of time. "Fuck me, that was close", said Ste.

We got a table seat and sat facing each other, Tim was reading the paper, Ste was admiring his new cards, Sam was checking his betting slip, and I was staring out the window wondering if we'd make the connecting train to Bolton. "Oh, Shit! you know what we've gone and forgot" said Sam, "No, what?" said Tim, "Some tinnies for the journey". "Ah, shit, yeah, we should have stopped at the offy on the way down to the station", "We're gonna have to wait until we get to Bolton now," said Ste. But I had a bit of a cunning surprise tucked away. I slowly put my hand into the inside pocket of my jacket where I had craftily concealed a bottle of Brandy. I'd originally planned to have it at the gig, but as this was now looking like an emergency... I revealed the bottle in the style of

'Eddie Hitler' from the sitcom Bottom, with a big "Ah ha, look what I've just found", "Koe you fuckin' beauty" shouted the lads all at once. We all shared the bottle, passing it around and having a good swig while we headed to Leeds.

We arrived at Leeds station and managed to get the connecting train to Bolton with hardly any time to spare, and were all now in good spirits, literally, and looking forward to getting to the gig. When we arrived in Bolton, you could tell Oasis was in town, there were loads of Liam wannabes strolling around and crowds of people bustling in pretty much every pub beer garden. We made a beeline for what looked like a decent traditional real ale pub, got a round of drinks in, and then sat down with a bunch of lads from Manchester. One of them shouted over, "You lads going to the gig?", "We've got some spare tickets if you want to buy some", Yeah, "but we don't need a ticket", said Tim, "We're on the guest list". "Yeah right", said the lads. They didn't believe us, but we continued chatting away and had a few beers with them. Then we all walked up to the Reebok Stadium together with them continually trying to flog their spare tickets to us.

When we arrived, it was heaving with people outside, but the doors weren't open yet and probably weren't going to be open for a few more hours. We found the box office and gave our names over the counter. A young lady started looking through the guest list. Meanwhile, the Mancunians were still with us, still not believing we were on the guest list and were doing their best to tout their tickets to us. "Erm... can't seem to find your names," said the lady, "Your names are not on our list". We were all now thinking, SHIT what if Jason had forgotten or if there'd been an error? We'd look a right set of dicks in front of these lads, but then, the lady said, are you The Undecided? "YES," we all said at once. She then produced an envelope with our tickets inside and an extra special surprise. "Looks like you're all in Hospitality," she said, giving us each a wristband. This meant we could enter the stadium immediately and not have to queue outside; it also allowed us entry into the VIP bar. "Fuckin' jackpot," shouted Sam, "Jason, you're an absolute star," shouted Ste. We made our way into the stadium and gave a royal wave to the Manchester lads who now had to join the queues outside with everyone else.

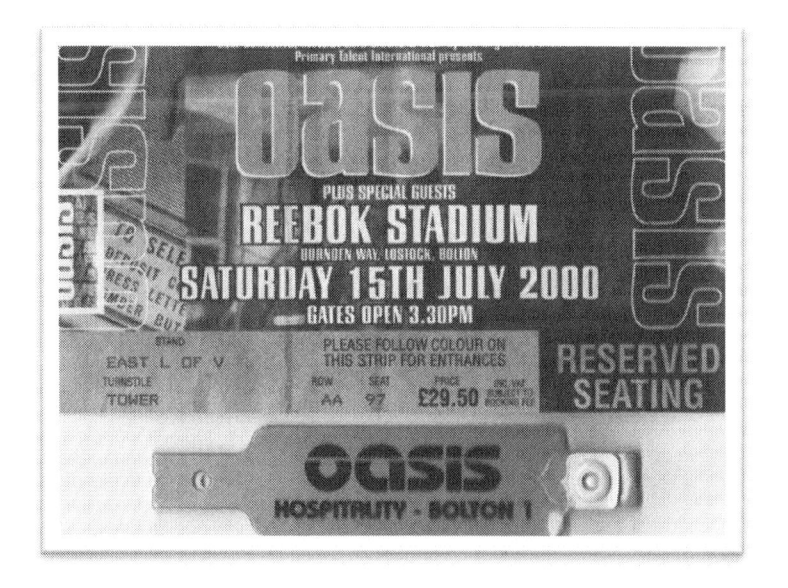

As we got inside and up to the top of the stairs, we were ushered into the VIP lounge and found that we were the first guests to arrive. It was a big room that had a bar at one side, and then the balcony overlooking the stadium at the other. What a view we had. We headed for the bar and were told the first hour of drinks was free, then they would be chargeable after that. I think this was meant so that each VIP guest would get at least one free drink on arrival, but we were on a session, so just put a big order in and then filled a table full of pints in one corner of the lounge.

It was time to chill, drink merrily, and wait for the gig to start. "Has anyone got any cigs left?" Said Sam, "I've only a few left". We all rummaged in our pockets and had maybe half a packet between us. "Right, we need to try to find a cigarette machine" I replied. Sam went to ask at the bar, and they pointed over to the far corner of the room which we'd not yet explored. Tim, Ste and I continued to chat and noticed more guests arriving, one of which Ste seemed to recognise. "Hey, I know that guy over there," said Ste, who then got up and sidled towards him. It was James Redmond, who played the character 'Finn' in the TV soap opera 'Hollyoaks'. More guests were arriving, so Tim and I also went to have a mingle to see who else was here with us.

I noticed a guy I recognised off the Television, he was on the music quiz show 'Never Mind the Buzzcocks' a few weeks prior, so I went over to chat to him. "Alright mate" I said, "Now I'm sure I recognise you off the tele?". "Alright, yeah, I've been on TV a few times mate, my name is John Robb". "Do I know you?" he said. "I'm Koe, I'm here with my band The Undecided, have you heard of us?" Obviously knowing he hadn't. "Er, yeah I think so, are you from Leeds?" I think he was being polite. "Nearby," I said, "We're from Keighley". "Ah, yeah, near Bradford", "Yeah that's the place" I said. "What do you play in the band?", he asked, "Bass guitar", to which he said, "I'm a bass player too". We continued to have a pretty good chat, he was telling me about his time when he was in a band called 'The Membranes' in the 1980s and that he'd recently written a biography of The Stone Roses. I was impressed and felt I needed to know more about this guy.

Tim came over and I introduced him to John, he knew him too from the tele. We were all getting on well, then Sam arrived back from the cigarette machine, and without any filter or warning, shouted over to John. "What the fuck are you wearing!?, You look like Crocodile Dundee". What an introduction, not! Just to explain, John was wearing a shiny faux reptile skin jacket. John looked at us as if to say, "Who the hell's this tosser?". "Oh, he's alright, this is Sam, our guitarist," said Tim. "He's a bit pissed". "No, I'm not!" said Sam, "I can see what he's wearing, and it looks way too shiny in my honest opinion, where on Earth did you get it from?". "I picked it up from a charity shop, only cost a tenner" said John, "Ok a tenner's not bad" replied Sam, "But how much did you spend on varnish?". John was obviously taken aback by what Sam had to say but stood his ground and laughed it off before leaving to go speak to other guests. "Nice one Sam, always one to make a good impression," I said.

"So, anyway Sam, did you manage to get some cigs?" said Tim. "Sure did, come over here and look what I found". So, we followed Sam over to the other side of the room where the cigarette machine was, and we noticed why Sam had been; let's say distracted for the past half hour. Stood at either side of the cigarette vending machine were two pretty, fit, young female models dressed in Marlborough branded low-cut top jumpsuits. "So, this is what you've been up to then Sam," said Tim, "Yeah, and I've already got one of their phone numbers" replied Sam. The girls were there to help us VIPs choose a packet from the machine and help us put our money in, which I guess was a bit of a marketing gimmick. Brilliant! After another half an hour of trying to chat up these young ladies and choosing from the range of cigarettes they had to offer, mainly 'Marlborough' obvs, we ended up with a few packs each and headed back to our table of drinks.

More guests were arriving. Tim noticed a guy with what looked like a tea cosy on his head. "I think I know him," said

Tim, so he went over to chat with him. Sam and I went to find Ste who was still chatting to James Redmond at the bar and trying his best to get his autograph for his girlfriend Jennie. As I looked around the room, which was now filling up, it dawned on me, that everyone in there was a celebrity in one way or another, people off the television like Vernon Kay and Tess Daly, Radio DJ's, and music industry big wigs, sports personalities including Rob Jones who played for Liverpool FC and England, and then there was us, The Undecided, who nobody knew. But! At the same time, they must have thought the same as us in some way, so we had to play on that we were some music artists on the cusp of stardom, and not just a bunch of piss artists from Keighley. Easier said than done!

I decided to head over to Tim to see who he was talking to. He was a bearded guy with a wool beanie hat on, which I thought, Fuckin' 'Ell, he must be hot in that, it's the middle of summer. "Koe, this is Damon," said Tim, "Alright mate, how are you doing Damon". "Yeah, I'm alright". "Who's this?" he said to Tim, "This is Koe, our bass player". "Are you in the music industry?" I said, "Erm, yeah, I go by the name Badly Drawn Boy". Now at this point, I had no idea who Badly Drawn

Boy was. We started chatting about our band and how we'd ended up at the gig, and then he told us that he'd released a few EPs and had just launched his debut album. After a good hour or so of setting the world to rights with Damon, it was time for the show.

We all got ushered outside onto the balcony and into our seats. The stadium was rammed, the fans all chanting for the support band to come on, who were none other than Happy Mondays. Shaun Ryder, Bez, and the gang were all on form and properly warmed up the crowd with their energetic early 90s indie classics. Then it was time for Oasis. The place was properly buzzing now, the intro music started blasting out, and what a belter to make a stage entrance to 'Fuckin' in the bushes', it sounded well ace, then out pops Noel and Liam and the rest of the band, and away they went with their first song 'Go Let It Out', with the crowd all singing along.

Now, I'd seen Oasis a few times before and had attended their Knebworth gig with Sam and my mate Lee Bilbrough in 1996. It was the best gig I'd ever been to in my honest opinion, it was probably the biggest crowd I'd ever witnessed. I read that 250,000 people attended that weekend. I recall, me and Sam nearly being run over by Liam Gallagher in a golf buggy he was driving through the crowd with Patsy Kensit sat shotgun and John Squire from The Stone Roses sat in the back seat with a bodyguard. Sam then called Liam a 'cunt' to his face, to which Liam jumped up out of his seat and started shouting back at him. The bodyguard had to restrain Liam and keep him calm. Sam ended up running off and climbing up this huge tree in the middle of the crowd and remained up there for the whole gig. The problem was, he struggled to get back down, and he was extremely late back for the coach. Me and Lee, plus the rest of the coach party had to wait an extra couple of hours for Sam to return, we were not best pleased as you can imagine. But I digress. **Back at the Reebok Stadium, I was looking forward to Oasis playing some new songs from their latest album 'Standing on the Shoulder of Giants', which they did and was superb! They played a blinding set finishing with 'Live Forever', but then coming back to encore with 'Champagne Supernova' and 'Rock n Roll Star'. We were all buzzing by now and headed back inside to refresh at the bar.**

As we filtered back indoors, it looked like all the celebs had the same idea and the bar was crammed. We waited our turn and decided to avoid having to queue every time by purchasing a bottle of red wine each to see the rest of the night through and headed back to our table in the corner. Jason popped up to see us all and had a drink with us, it was good to see him and have a catch-up after the show, he told us that he had our new 'Like a Dove' album playing backstage before the gig and the lads liked a couple of our songs, which was nice to hear. We thanked him for inviting us to the gig and getting us into Hospitality before he headed back to finish sorting out the gear backstage. We chatted a bit more with John Robb* and Damon too, reflecting on the gig before they headed off. Ste gave Damon one of his newly printed business cards and asked him to keep in touch**.

The room slowly emptied, with only a few die-hard drinkers left, including us. Then suddenly, more people entered the room, it was the Happy Mondays minus Shaun Ryder. They got a round of drinks in and sat around a table in the middle of the room. By this time, the wine had kicked in on top of the many beers we'd had throughout the day, and it showed. Ste and Sam started dancing around the table where Bez, Rowetta and the rest of the Happy Mondays were sitting, whilst Tim and I were watching from afar. They looked like a cross between Mick Jagger and Paul Calf in the way they were moving. It was hilarious but I wasn't sure if The

Happy Mondays thought the same. I decided to go over and rescue them. I sat down next to Bez, "You guys were brilliant tonight" I said, "Alright mate, cheers" he said, "Are these guys with you?", "Yeah, these are my guitarists from my band The Undecided" I replied. "They're fuckin' mental aren't they", "More mental than me and Shaun", I laughed, "Yeah, we've had a long day out on the beer, where's Shaun by the way?" "Ah, he went off somewhere with Liam and left us here mate". He then dipped into the pocket of his long beige rain mac, pulled out a bunch of Chupa Chup lolly pops and handed them to me, "Ere mate, have one of these, and give your mates one". "Cheers, nice one mate". I think that may have been a polite way of telling us to bugger off.

I gathered Ste and Sam, gave them their lolly pops and we went and sat back at our table to polish off our bottles of wine. Soon, the Happy Mondays left, and the final few people all disappeared from the room. The bar staff were all finishing off clearing up and then left a short while after. Then there was just us four left, steaming away in the corner, necking the last few dregs out of our wine bottles at a table full of empty glasses and an ashtray full of tab ends that had started billowing out.

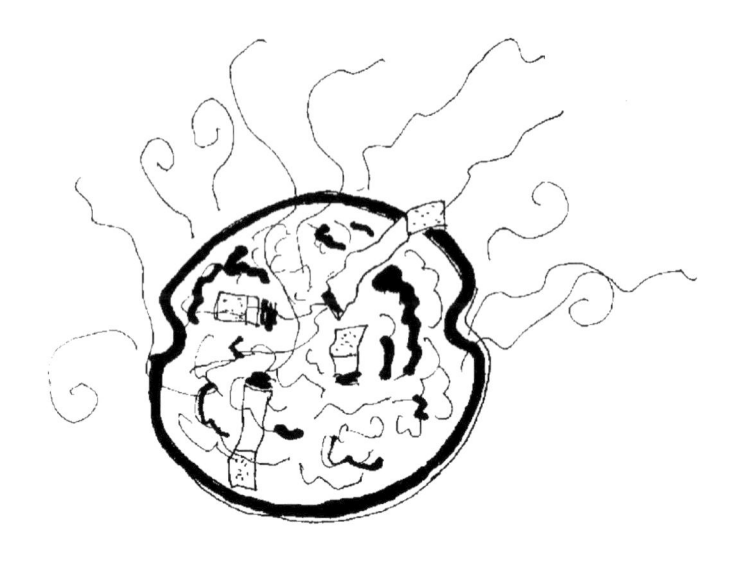

A security guard approached us and said, "Right then lads, it looks like it's just you left in here, and I'm going to have to ask you to leave so we can lock up". We all got up and wobbled over to the exit, gingerly made our way back down the stairs and out the door we came in about 10 hours earlier. "Night lads," said the security guard, then the door shut behind us and the stadium lights turned off.

We gazed out across the vast empty carpark outside, it was desolate, just a load of empty beer cups and burger wrappers blowing around in circles like mini tornadoes. "What time is it?" said Sam, "2 am," I said, "Haha 2 am", replied Sam, then we all started singing our song 2am. "How the fuck are we going to get home?" said Ste, "No idea," I said, "We've missed the last train, and we'll probably have to get a taxi". We didn't have a mobile phone with us and couldn't ring a taxi, so we had no option but to slowly stumble back into Bolton and try to find a taxi rank.

As we started staggering across the carpark, we noticed some headlights moving towards us. As they got nearer, we spotted that it was a Transit van. "Hey, let's flag it down," said Sam. So, we all started waving and flapping about. The van screeched up in front of us and a young Asian lad popped his head out of the window. "Alright lads, what you up to" he said. "Can you give us a lift into Bolton?" said Tim. "Is that where you're from" he replied, "No, we're from Keighley near Bradford". "Ah, yeah, I know where that is, I've a cousin over that way", "I could give you a lift to Bradford if you want, but you'll have to chip in for some petrol and that". "How much do you want?" we asked, "call it £60". We all looked at each other and nodded, "Have we got that much left between us?" We coppered up and found we were pretty much £59 short.

"Can you take us to a cash machine first?" said Ste, "Erm, yeah, ok" replied the van driver. We all jumped into the back of the van and set off. When we got to the cash machine in Bolton town centre, we noticed an Indian takeaway next door. "I'm hungry", said Sam, "I could murder a curry," said Tim. We asked if it was alright to wait while we ordered some food, and the driver agreed.

30 minutes later and now approaching 3 am, we set off towards Bradford. So, there we were, all sat on the floor in the back of a Transit van, driven by a total stranger, whilst eating curry from a tray, and bouncing up and down at a rate of knots, cruising down the M62 towards Yorkshire. He ended up driving us all to our front doors before he headed off to see his cousin. What a great guy, and what a stroke of luck we had at the end of an almighty session.

*A few years later I bumped into John Robb at another Oasis gig in Manchester, again in Hospitality and we reminisced. I kept in touch on Facebook via his 'Louder Than War' music magazine, which then led me to the opportunity to meet him in Leeds. It was at his new book launch tour for 'The Art of Darkness' where he agreed to write the forward to this book.

**Unfortunately, Damon didn't call us back then, only a short while after we had met him, his debut album 'The Hour of the Bewilderbeast' won the Mercury Music Prize and his career took off. But many years later, during

SIXTEEN DRUMMERS – THE STORY OF **THE UNDECIDED**

Lockdown he was pretty active on Twitter and Tim had commented on things that led to him and Damon following each other. Tim wrote a dm to Damon saying "Sorry to intrude into your personal messages but do you remember chatting at the Oasis gig in Bolton?"...he said "Absolutely fine and yes I do remember you"...He put a photo of Frank Sidebottom Christmas baubles on one of his Twitter posts and Tim sent a dm to ask where he got them (he got them off actual Frank)...not long after that Damons brother had sadly passed away and Tim sent him another dm to send his best to him and his family, which he answered with a long message thanking Tim.

Not long after, Tim got unwell and was battling with Cancer, he told Damon that he might not be on Twitter much, and from then on Damon sent Tim a personal message every Friday right up to his last operation, which was very nice of him.

SIXTEEN DRUMMERS – THE STORY OF **THE UNDECIDED**

John Robb and I finally managed to catch up – The Old Woolen, Farsley - 2024

CHAPTER 5
GIVE AND TAKE

GRAND THEFT AUTO

After several months of rest, we started looking for a new drummer again. My dad mentioned a lad at his work called Gregg Lewis, who played the drums and said he could ask him if he'd like to join the band, to which I said, "Yeah, no harm in trying, let's give him an audition". The next week, my dad asked Gregg, and he agreed to give us a try. We all met up at the practice rooms located in an old mill in Keighley. Sam, Ste, Tim, and I arrived first to set up our gear, and waited for Gregg to arrive.

He turned up not long after, but he didn't know where to go with his drum kit, so he came in to find us first. We were all up on the top floor of a mill where we were now practising. He made his way upstairs and eventually found us through the labyrinth of corridors and popped his head in to check he had the right place. "Alright lads", said Gregg, "Alright Gregg, good to meet you", we replied. "Where's your drum kit" asked Ste, "Ah, it's down in my car, I didn't want to cart it up here and find it was the wrong place, any chance you can give us a hand to bring it up here?" "Yeah, no worries" we replied.

The practice room we had was quite a way from the carpark and adjoining street, so carting all the gear from our cars to the practice room was a bit of a farce, especially carrying drum kits.

We all made our way back downstairs and onto the side street where Gregg had parked his car. When we got to it, we noticed his car door was already open and on looking into the car it was empty. "FUCK!" shouted Gregg, "Some fuckers nicked my kit". "Fucking' Ell man," said Ste, "Ah shit," said the rest of us. "What are we going to do now? Was it expensive?" said Ste, "Yeah, it was a brand-new Pearl Masters kit and cost me two grand". "Oh, shit man, we better call the cops" I replied.

Gregg phoned the Police and reported the theft. He was quite obviously pissed off with what had happened, and we were all annoyed at the situation for Gregg, his first audition with us starting like this, which pretty much left us all up shit creek without a paddle. But we were kindly offered to use another band's kit to practice with for the evening. "Are you alright with still having a practice with us Gregg if we can borrow a kit?" said Ste, "I suppose so, yeah, fuck it, let's do this" replied Gregg.

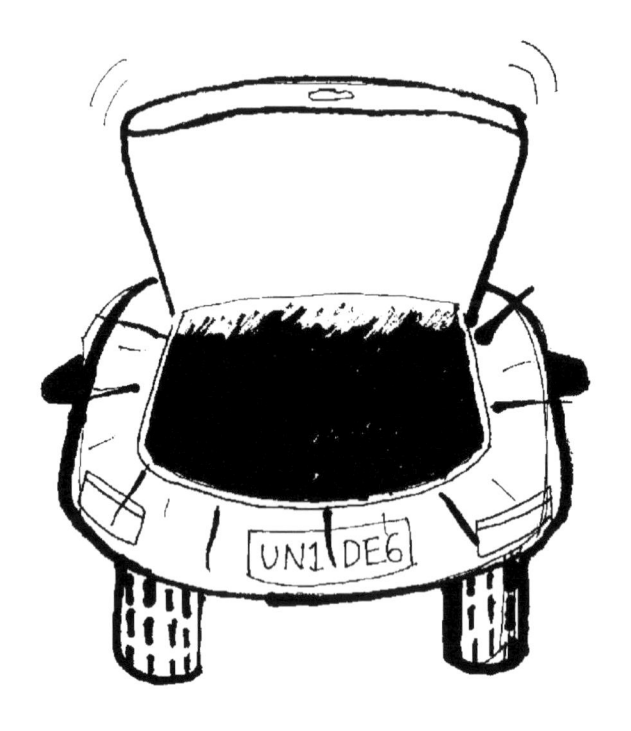

And so, we introduced our set of songs, to which he drummed away with ease. He picked them up with no problem and we managed to find some positive vibes to end the evening. The next morning, I contacted David Knights at the Keighley News, and he wrote an article about the theft in the next issue of the newspaper and asked the readers to be on the lookout for the kit, though it was never found.

SIXTEEN DRUMMERS – THE STORY OF **THE UNDECIDED**

Gregg eventually got a replacement drum kit and continued to be our drummer for the next few months. We played another gig at The British Legion in Haworth and then one at Gregg's local pub The Martins Nest in Brighouse, before heading out to play our only Manchester gig at The Roadhouse* on Newton Street, Piccadilly. We ended up getting on the bill there via a band called Western Suburbs, with whom Gregg had a stint as drummer before playing with us. That was unfortunately our last gig with Gregg and our last gig of 2001 before we took a year out.

*The Roadhouse in Manchester was another venue like that of The Duchess, or The Trades Club where many well-known bands had played around the same time as us, such as Elbow, Muse, Coldplay and The White Stripes to name but a few. Sadly, the venue closed in 2015. *Source: Wikipedia*

WORKING CLASS HEROES

Continuing into the Summer of 2001, we paused our rehearsals and gigging shortly after Gregg had left the band. We didn't want to rush back into booking any more gigs and then scrambling about like crazy to source a drummer. Instead, we went our separate ways for a bit. Tim moved to Ireland and ended up working in a Kebab shop in Sligo called 'Abrakebabra', which didn't last long, so he moved back and started a covers band with Ste called 'For A Few Dollars More'. Sam joined a few other mates to form a new band called Wet Paint, whilst I believe it or not, ended up joining a soul band with Gregg and his girlfriend Cheryl. We practised in the same building as In A City studio, playing some quite funky covers and were not far off gigging, but we ended up parting ways and that was the end of that, which left me at a bit of a loose end. I wasn't prepared to do any solo work at the time but wanted to keep doing something in music and thought, if I'm not going to perform then I'll help other musicians and bands with their music, and with that, I formed 'Koe Music'.

Koe Music was a music promotion and production company, that helped bands and musicians promote their music online as the Internet was in full swing by then, it was the .com boom, though not many bands knew how to get their music online, so a helping hand was what I gave them. I pretty much went all in, two-footed and invested £1000s of my own money into the company. I built a website from the ground up to showcase all the upcoming band's music, a kind of Myspace with extras. I was attending as many gigs as I could locally, gathering music recordings and then giving the bands some space on my website. I promoted the website via the local newspapers, radio, and via my contacts that I had already established with The Undecided. I had flyers, posters, and even ruddy car stickers printed up. At one point I had bands from all around the country sending in material, I even had a band follow me in my car (they'd seen the car sticker in my rear window), then trailed after me for miles from Newcastle back into Yorkshire, when I stopped for a break, they pounced on me and gave me a CD. It was surreal.

After gathering together an albums-worth of the recordings, I decided to create a compilation CD to showcase the bands. I invested in a multi-CD recorder that could record four CDs at a time and created a few hundred copies, then designed the sleeve and packaged them up for distribution.

The CDs were sold for £10 each and the proceeds after costs, were paid to my chosen charity Sue Ryder Care at the Manorlands Hospice in Oxenhope. I managed to raise a good few hundred pounds for them over the following year, and the bands received promotions on my website and in the local newspapers.

The compilation CDs were titled, Working Class Heroes*. Volume 1 was released at the back end of 2001 whilst the follow-up volume 2, was released in summer 2002. They included songs from the likes of:

The Undecided, Western Suburbs, Montauk Island, Stonefish, Kief Lloyd, Episonic, Slider, Circus?, Fake Uzi, DJ Tempest, Barcode, Schrödinger's Cat, Artimesia, Hush, Johnny and the Poorboys, Deepfill, and Fluke Shot Frenzy.

*Working Class Heroes compilation albums can be found online at the following SoundCloud link:

https://soundcloud.com/user-217214604

DRANK THE PLACE DRY

After nearly 18 months away from the band, we regrouped and started to practice again as we'd found our tenth drummer Daniel Green. He was another youngster compared to us maybe only 14 or 15 years old, but he was a brilliant drummer and managed to tolerate our drinking and the banter that went with it. Dan's first gig with us was an absolute belter. It was back at our usual stomping ground, The British Legion in Haworth and we had support from Wet Paint and Circus?.

The gig was a pay-on-the-door gig, but whoever we put on the door to take the money must have forgotten how many people they could let in due to the restricted capacity, and pretty much allowed everyone in! It was packed to the rafters, probably the busiest that the venue has ever been, and was way over capacity, but we weren't complaining. Wet Paint were up first and played an impressive mix of well-known covers in their own style which went down well and warmed up the crowd. Next up was Circus? who put in the usual mix of their Grunge originals and some Nirvana classics, which got the crowd moshing about. Then it was our turn on stage, and with having a bit of time out recently, and having a brand-new drummer with only a few practices under his belt, the nerves started to set in.

Before coming out onto the stage, we played our usual and now popular intro music 'La resa dei conti' composed by Ennio Morricone. It was used in the Sergio Leone film 'For a Few Dollars More'. It's the one that starts with the pocket watch chime and builds into a crescendo of trumpets. We then joined in and merged into 'The Score'.

We got off to a good start and the crowd was well behind us, we did have a bit of a rocky middle section when it came to some slower numbers, so we decided to split our set in two to have a break in between, and it was at this point that we got the message from the club manager, Roy, that they were running out of beer.

The social club downstairs was also more busy than usual and due to us having an over-capacity crowd upstairs who were all drinking like fish, the beer barrels and bottles were starting to deplete. As soon as everyone caught wind of that, they all rushed to the bar and ordered what they could. Before we could finish our second set, the club had completely run out of beer and the punters had to resort to whatever was left. We were ok though as we still had our beer rider in the backstage room, as we'd learned over the years to take our own drinks as backup. For us, the gig was a success, we'd taken hundreds on the door which we split between the bands, and we also managed to raise some cash for the Manorlands Hospice.

The following day we returned to the club to collect our gear. When we arrived, Roy was super pissed with us, and so were the Sunday regulars who had to resort to a mishmash of cider, shots, and pop instead of their regular lager and beer whilst watching the Sunday football. We just shrugged our shoulders and suggested they buy more beer in future if they have bands on upstairs. Roy was a nice guy and kind of caught between a rock and a hard place really, he had the regular's expectations to manage and then us, and he loved his music and live bands playing, so he didn't want to get into any arguments. He let it go and agreed he'd make sure the club stocked more beer before any future gigs.

PLUGGING AWAY

Continuing with my music promotion and production company Koe Music, I had a new idea. It was my next promotional CD to plug local talent, which also had advertising space on the inner sleeve for local businesses and events. This allowed for some sponsorship towards the production costs of the CD, and better still, allowed it to be free to the public. I called it 'Hear Plug'.

I released 3 issues of the Hear Plug CD between 2002 and 2003 which contained songs from the likes of:

Stonefish, The Undecided, Hush, Johnny and the Poorboys, Fluke Shot Frenzy, Tha Operator, Circus?, Barcode, Fugoo, Powder Monkeys, The Pipers, The Adventures of B Violet, Western Suburbs, Schrödinger's Cat, Operator 6, Cosmic Cuppa, Bloodstream, Threshold Shift, Skeletal Family, Pocketsize, Montauk Island.

When I released the first issue, I distributed them to local shops and record stores, pubs, and clubs. The first batch started to go quickly. But after a few weeks, the uptake slowed down, and I had a few hundred copies left and needed a way to shift them all to good homes for the benefit of the bands and the sponsors. I decided to re-launch them at a music open day, which was a bit of family fun throughout the daytime and a gig in the evening to showcase some of the bands on the CD.

I hired out the upstairs room of The Parkside Club in Haworth (formerly known as The British Legion) for the whole day. I then advertised the event in the local newspapers and put posters up around the village. I even had my kid brother Adam handing out the flyers to the tourists on Main Street. We had music stalls, Merchandise, a Raffle and Tombola, and a DJ playing music during the daytime. My family and friends helped me out and we had a steady stream of people coming and going. The music open day was fairly successful and made a few hundred pounds for the kitty, and shifted a good number of the Hear Plug CDs.

The evening event was much busier and pretty much on par with the time we'd drank the place dry, though we had to stick to the capacity on this one due to stricter fire regulations and agreed to run it as a ticket-only gig. Supporting The Undecided that night, newcomers 'Cosmic Cuppa' followed by 'Operator 6', which was their debut performance and was very popular with the crowd*. They were followed up by our close comrades 'Wet Paint' and 'Circus?' before the penultimate band 'Powder Monkeys' took to the stage. The Undecided completed the line-up, and we rocked with our usual set. It was a successful event all-round and enjoyed by all. I did manage to record some of the live songs from the night, which appear on the second issue of the Hear Plug CDs.

After the launch event, I started to gain more publicity for the Hear Plug CD and more bands submitted their music. I also started getting complimentary tickets to gigs being sent to my house. One of which was sent by Roger Nowell and Stan Greenwood of the well-known Keighley Goth Rock band 'Skeletal Family'. I'd known Roger via Jason Rhodes as he worked alongside him as a bass guitar technician with Oasis. The ticket I received from them was for a Skeletal Family gig at The New Variety Club (Gas Club) 'Gasienda' to the locals in Keighley. They had a special guest support band called 'The Dogs', who at the time, no one really knew. But believe it or not, included Bonehead from Oasis on Rhythm Guitar, and Mike Joyce from The Smiths on Drums; two rock idles in my mind and I had the pleasure of meeting them and having a chat after their set. It was a great night and the first time I'd seen Skeletal Family play, who were superb. After that, I added their song 'Promised Land' to the next issue of the Hear Plug CD.

Another complementary ticket I received was for a band playing at Pennington's Variety Club in Bradford. They were called Dead Men Walking and were a kind of supergroup made up of some well-known Punk/Goth Rock band members; Glen Matlock (Sex Pistols), Mike Peters (The Alarm), Kirk Brandon (Spear of Destiny) and Billy Duffy (The Cult). It was another fantastic gig and another great perk of running a music promotions company.

The second and third issues of the Hear Plug CD were distributed until every copy found a new home. Unfortunately, there wasn't to be a fourth issue. I had pretty much depleted all my funds in making the CDs, and with the uptake of the Internet moving much quicker that year and MP3 players becoming all the rage, I was facing a losing battle as CDs were slowly becoming unpopular with people favouring digital downloads, it was a sign of the times.

To end this story on a high, I'd like to mention a little gig we did for a school in Bradford. I'm not sure which school it was, or how we ended up playing there, all we can remember is that Sam probably arranged it with the teachers, maybe through his dad. I recall we all rocked up to the school, including a mate of ours, Michael 'Boy' Reddiough who supported on additional guitar. We set up on a stage in the main school hall. The teachers then led all the kids towards the stage in single file and sat them down in front of us like a school assembly. We played a load of Oasis and Beatles songs and a few of our own for them, and they absolutely loved it. They thought we were mega stars and queued for autographs after our performance, it was nice. Legend has it that either the singer Gareth Gates or even the magician Dynamo was one of the kids in the audience, though I am not too sure.

*Operator 6 continued with their popularity and supported some well-known artists such as Ocean Colour Scene and Paul Weller.

My dad, Nick helping at the Hear Plug music open day - Parkside Club,

Haworth - 2003

TOUCH AND GO

It was the summer of 2004, and we'd always wanted to play an open-air festival in a field, instead of the indoor festivals we had already performed at. Back then, there weren't many music festivals in the North of England. We did have the Leeds music festival at Bramham Park, and we also had a more local music festival at Myrtle Park in Bingley called 'Music at Myrtle' (which later became 'Bingley Music Live'). We never had the chance to play at these as they weren't as accessible for unsigned bands as festivals are today.

An opportunity came about for us to appear at a local homemade outdoor festival, which was organised by Sam and the guys from Wet Paint, and members of another local band called The Culprits. They'd secured a location that was distant from any houses where you'd get noise complaints etc and had a pub nearby for obvious reasons. It was to be held in a field at the side of The Guide Inn, up on the hilltops between Keighley and Cullingworth. They called the festival 'Guide Fest'.

For the stage, they had this open-back trailer from an

articulated lorry which was supplied by a local haulage firm. They had a decent PA and mixing desk set up and run by an old mate from Haworth, Stephen 'Smiggy' Smith. The festival was run as a charity event and all proceeds were going to the Manorlands hospice in Oxenhope, which as you know from reading this book, is close to the hearts of many of us from these parts, a very worthy cause and one we all took pride in performing for over the years.

The Undecided were asked to open the festival, which was an honour, but was also pretty much touch and go as Tim had just arrived back in the UK from his trip to Cuba and ended up coming straight from the airport to sing. He got there just in the nick of time. It was 2 pm on a Saturday, hot and sunny and we had a decent crowd standing in front of us in the fields. The gig went down a treat and we stayed to watch all the other bands perform through the afternoon and into the hazy evening, what a glorious day it was. The other bands that performed at the festival were: Ironstorm, Angel Chain, Circus?, Nexus, Random Hand, and The Culprits.

SIXTEEN DRUMMERS – THE STORY OF **THE UNDECIDED**

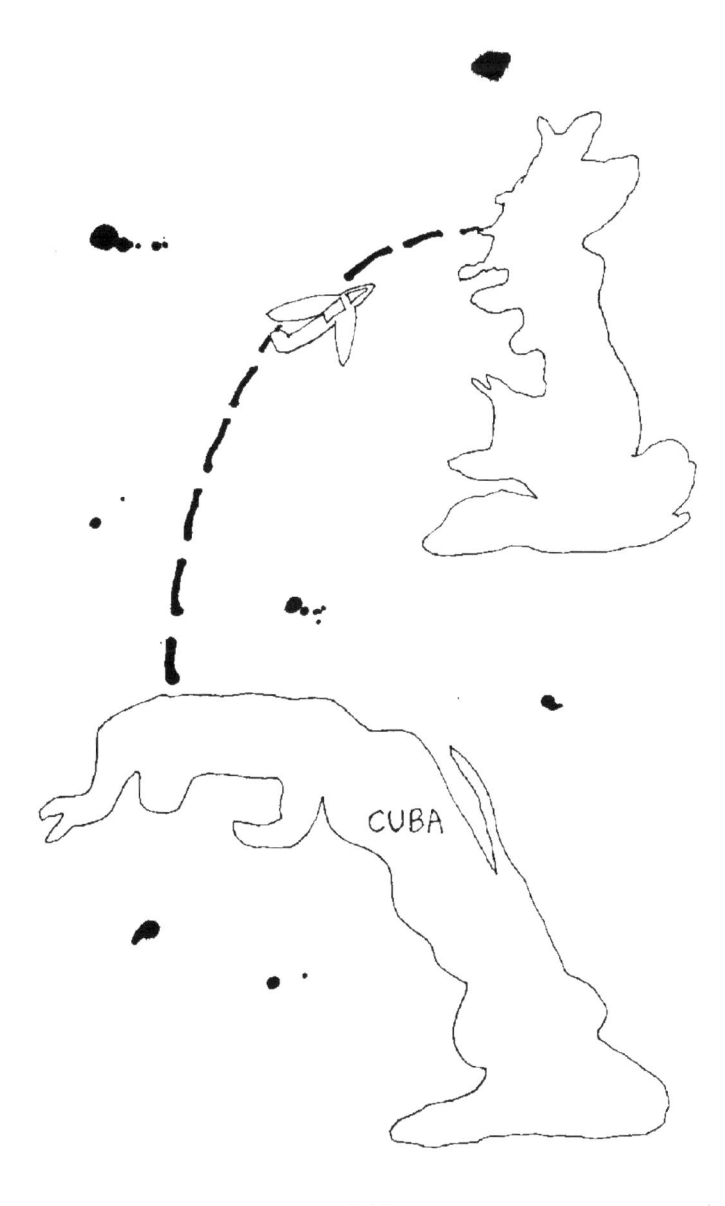

Guide Fest was our last gig for a few years as not only had Dan left the band to further his music career*, Ste and I had started new families and had kids to raise, Tim had returned to Cuba, and Sam continued gigging with Wet Paint and another band called Get Guns before he too started a family. It was for the time, the end of The Undecided and the end of an era, but we always kept in touch with the thought that one day we'd all be back.

*Daniel Green did go far with his music career and is now the head of academic development at the ICMP (The Institute of Contemporary Music Performance) based in London. He also provides his knowledge of music in the 'Musicology' feature on the BBC Radio 6 Music – Huw Stephens show.

CHAPTER 6

THE LATER YEARS

BEATS AND BARMINESS

Fast forward to 2009, and after taking a few years out to raise kids and spending time with our families, we regrouped as The Undecided once again. We were still lacking a drummer and were holding auditions again. A few drummers came and went in the process and to be honest, they didn't make the grade, we can't even remember their names, that's how bad they were. But one person that did become available to us was the singer/guitarist from Wet Paint, 'Luke Parker' who by now was a good drummer too and offered to be our new stickman number Sixteen.

We had a new practice room too, which was at the local Community Centre in Haworth, but this time we did have permission, not like back in 1995 when Monty and Sam had the run-in with the caretaker. Luke was familiar with most of our songs already as he'd played alongside us with other bands over the years and got to know the beats for them. We also threw in a few new songs which cemented the band further, and our first few practice sessions were almost gig-worthy. It wasn't too long before we started gigging again. One gig stood out on the calendar for us, it was the 'Beat-Herder music festival'. Back then, we'd only heard the odd rumour bandied about here and there about the festival, as though it was like the best kept secret, and by invitation only to a select few. So, when Luke told us that he worked there and had been asked for us to play there, we were all up for it without question.

It was the afternoon of the gig, and we all bundled into Ste's van. It was one of those Bedford Rascals / Suzuki Carry vans or 'Sooty Van' if you like. It was a bit of a tight squeeze with all the gear though. (Let me put it this way, those vans are that small, one time Ste looked out of his living room window and thought someone had nicked it, but it turned out it was parked behind a lamp post). But as you know we'd experienced this kind of thing before, and the contortionist-act skills we'd learned over the years would have easily given the lovely Debbie Magee a run for her money.

We didn't have a clue where Beat-Herder was but aimed the van towards Clitheroe in Lancashire. As we drew nearer, we started to see many coloured flags waving in the distance and eventually emerging into view, a small town of tents, marquees, and fairground rides.

We'd arrived at the festival site and headed for the accreditation kiosk to receive the wristbands that would allow us entry into Beat-Herdershire. I recall as we were waiting in the queue, Ste and I spotted a mate of ours from Wilsden, Mark Hall*, dragging what looked like a standard 1980s 3-piece suite across a field, maybe he's moving in, I thought to myself, it was quite a spectacle.

Once we were in, we had a stroll down the main strip and headed towards the 'Beat-Herder & District Working Men's Social Club' which was where we were going to perform that evening. We arrived, and it was clear to see how it had got its name. It was certainly in the style of an old 1970s working men's club, all chintzy pub furnishings, a real ale bar, and some crazy cabaret in full swing on the stage at the back of the marquee. The atmosphere was giddy and electric, and we couldn't wait to play. We were ushered backstage to get our gear ready, tune up and prep for our performance. Back then, the backstage area was just a small empty marquee, but over the years, the organisers have made improvements with some creature comforts of sofas, rugs and other fun fixtures and fittings, and is probably the best backstage area of the festival for bands to chill before and after performances.

We entered the stage and hit the crowd with a mix of our oldies and some new songs. It took a couple of songs to get the crowd warmed up, and one song, a new one we'd introduced to the set, got them going; 'Dance like a Gecko', as the title states, had them bouncing around all over the place. We only had a short set, maybe 30-40 minutes, but it was very enjoyable for us and the crowd.

After our gig, we stayed on to watch a guy called Captain Hotknives perform. He was brilliant, funny as fuck songs with crazy lyrics, but quite clever too. We then had a whistle-stop tour of the festival, taking in all the sights, smells, and sounds. For a first-timer, I was very much impressed with how things were set up, and how much attention to detail had been put into some of the stage areas, like Toil Trees, and the little village set up in the woods, complete with a bar, hotel, garage with cars you can dance on top of, a tattoo parlour and many weird and wonderful shops, before topping this off with a church, yes, that's right a church full of disco balls and ravers in the middle of a wood, it was as though we'd followed the white rabbit down the hole.

Unfortunately, we couldn't stay, we hadn't brought any camping gear and Ste and I both had work the next morning, which was a shame, though I'm sure Sam did go back the next day to stay for the rest of the weekend. Ste and I did return to perform there a few times with our next band Indianic, and I have been going ever since. It's a place of magic and wonderment and may it continue.

*Mark Hall later became the lead singer and songwriter for our next band incarnation Indianic.

ANYONE FOR CRICKET?

After playing our only summer gig at the Beat-Herder festival, we continued to write some new songs and jam regularly without being too bothered about booking any further gigs. We instead focused on getting enough new material together to make another recording. But come autumn 2009, we were approached to perform at a bit of a gathering at Keighley Cricket Club. We were a bit reluctant at first, but agreed to play, as they were raising some funds for the club, and we could at least test some of our new songs with an audience.

It was the night of the gig, we all turned up, but some of us were a bit worse for wear and not in good shape to play. I had a terrible back problem, *still do*, but it had flared up and was giving me serious gip. I was on a ton of painkillers and wasn't sure if I could pick my guitar up, never mind playing it. Luke turned up with a seriously deep gash in his hand that he'd picked up at work, which was right across his palm, and he was in agony, he really should have gone to hospital. We were kind of in limbo as to whether to play or cancel the gig. We crazily decided to play.

After setting up all the gear, which took ages due to our condition, we then found that Luke simply couldn't hold one of his drumsticks due to the gash, which by now was just weeping, and looked like it needed stitches. "Why don't you play one-handed" said Sam. "Erm, I'm not sure that's going to work Sam", "Why not? the drummer from Def Leppard only has one arm and he can play drums" replied Sam. "Yeah but he's had years of practice, I can't just go from two hands to one hand in a night," said Luke. "So, what are we going to do," said Tim. "I know what we can do" said Ste, reaching into a box of cables, and other bits 'n' bobs of gig equipment. He pulled out a roll of Gaffer tape, and responded, "Let's tape the drumstick into his bad hand, then he won't need to grip it". "Yeah, it's worth a try," said Tim. Luke wasn't too sure and was shaking his head in amazement. "Here Luke, take some of these painkillers and strap up" I said, "It'll be alright, we can have a few whiskeys as well to mask the pain, I need it too for my back".

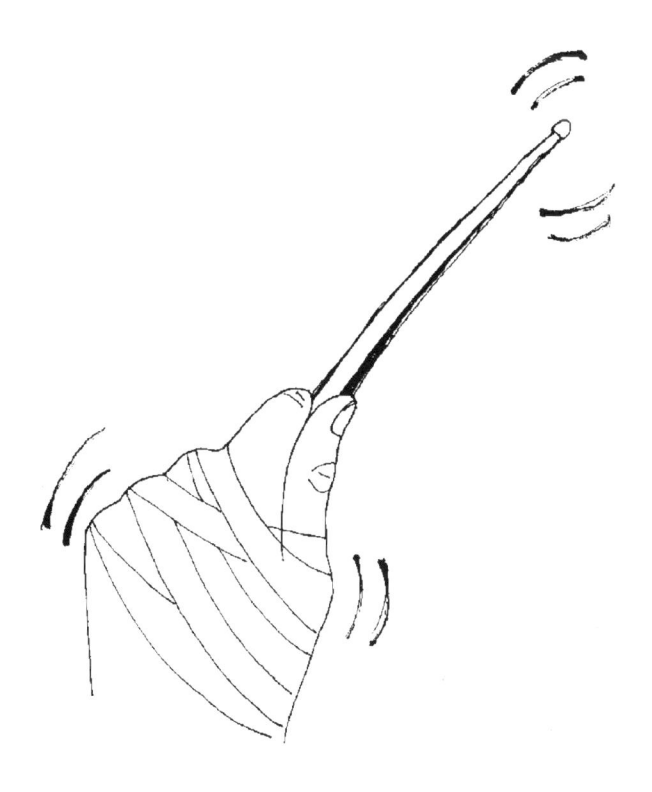

With a stick of hickory now strapped to Luke's hand, and the both of us starting to get high on a cocktail of Jamesons and Co-Codamol we proceeded to rock the joint. It started off ok, and we managed to get through a few songs unscathed, but as we got six or seven songs in, I started to wobble all over the place, I was pissed and spaced at the same time.

I turned around to see how Luke was doing, he had the eyes of a madman, sweating buckets and grimacing through the pain, he looked like we'd hooked him up to the mains electric supply.

We eventually managed to pull off a full set of songs and the feedback was positive, considering how much discomfort we were in. Afterwards, Luke carefully unpeeled the Gaffer tape from his hand which now looked gammy. We decided to have a few more whiskeys before calling it a night, heading home, and putting a lid on doing any further gigs for that year. Luke eventually got his hand looked at and made a full recovery.

JULIE

It was May 2010, and we'd got a handful of songs ready to record for an EP. We decided to use a studio in Idle, Bradford called IVOLV, which was situated in the basement of an old back street printers' workshop. My brother Pete had recommended IVOLV after recording some tracks there for his hip-hop outfit 'Ill Bass Method' the year before and put us in touch with the guy who ran the studio; 'Grant Henderson'. Grant was a top lad and an excellent music engineer, he also played drums for a band called Vinnie & The Stars. We spent a few days at the studio during May and managed to get 4 songs recorded. In between recording my bass guitar parts to each song, I'd be going back to work, then back to the studio again on an evening. On the final day of our recording, I finished work and promptly headed back to the studio to see how the rest of the lads had done in getting their guitar and singing tracks down.

I entered the building via an old metal door, it was like a coal hatch that led into the basement, then made my way through the warren of corridors to get to the studio rooms. When I got there, I noticed Grant, sitting at his mixing desk giggling to himself, I was wondering what was going on. I then noticed what looked like a woman with her back to me in long black boots and a white dress, she had long white straggly hair. She just stood there, fidgeting about behind a curtain that divided the rooms, she looked like she was adjusting her bra, then started messing around with her frontal bits, and I'm like "Who the fuck is that?" Then she turned around, "All right Koe", in a croaky, deeper voice than I was expecting; and fuckin' Ell, I nearly died. It was Sam, in a dress, wig and long boots. "What the hell are you doing dressed like that Sam?" I replied. "I'm not Sam, I'm Julie," he/she said. Grant then started laughing his head off to my dismay.

Earlier that day, whilst I was at work, all fun and games were rife. Sam had turned up to the studio as Julie and recorded his/her final guitar parts for our EP. But they didn't confine themselves to the studio, they only went out to the local pub around the corner, dressed scantily clad with a tissue-stuffed bra and a budgie-stuffed pair of pantyhose, joined by the rest of the gang. They told me about their antics and what Julie had got up to, which sounded hilarious, I'd missed a proper piss-funny afternoon. To set the record straight, Sam wasn't a trans and had nothing against them, he was just being as spontaneous as he always was, buggering about and having a bit of dressing-up fun.

Later, Julie changed clothes and we all got on with mixing down the recordings until we had some final mixes. The songs we recorded were: 'The Underclass', 'I Will Get By', 'Dance Like a Gecko' and 'Working Class Hero' (our take on the John Lennon classic). We named the EP Dance Like a Gecko and released it on CD, it was a very limited edition. We then added the songs to a best of The Undecided CD called '15 Years on and Still Rocking'. It was to be the final studio recording for The Undecided, and the last time we saw Julie.

CASTLE CAPERS

Following on from our session in the recording studio with Julie, we had been booked to play at a local music festival called 'The Aire Do'* which was held in the parks and grounds of Cliffe Castle in Keighley. It was a free festival put on by the Keighley Town Council and was by then in its fifth year. The main stage was set up on the park's large bandstand and they had a smaller stage set up in an adjoining marquee. The sound system was provided by the guys from the Beat-Herder festival. They boasted that it had the largest Magnolia-coloured speakers in the world.

We were the first band on, kick-starting the festival and we took to the smaller stage in the marquee. We had a good turnout, considering it was only 2 pm. Some of our usual followers were there in support, and we also had some new additions to our fanbase; Ste's sons, Harrison, and Oliver** and my son and daughter Lewie and Evie. I remember our Lewie grabbing a tambourine and jamming along with us, and dancing around, he loved it, and it made me feel on top of the world too.

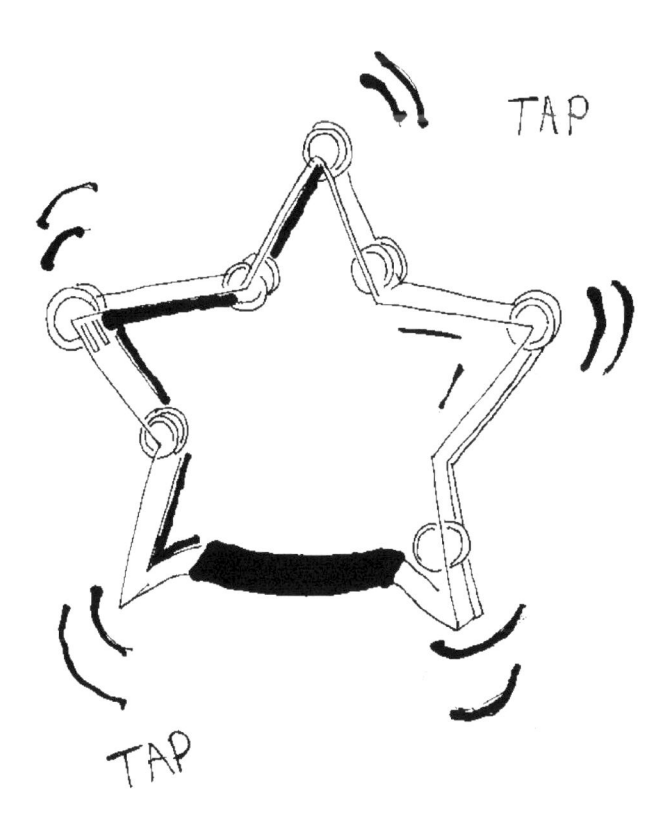

We played a mix of oldies and all the new songs we'd just recorded in the studio, which were well received.

After our performance, we stayed on through the afternoon and into the early evening to watch the rest of the show. The other bands that performed were Box Jellys, The

Lajpal Group (UK), Howling Johnny and The Full Moon Blues Band, Meet the Committee, Fifteen Stories, Father Hen, Revolver, Meet Me in Vegas, Arcomnia, DeLorean Drivers, and Lovely Eggs, with the headline act being Reverend and The Makers. It was a fantastic event for the local community and led to further Aire Do's for a few more years featuring other local bands like Foxes Faux and Rockbottom Risers, as well as some signed music artists like Rudimental and Jake Bugg.

The Aire Do festival was to be our only gig of 2010, and it was later during our next band practice that Tim announced he was hanging up his microphone and retiring from the band. It was a bit of a sad ending as we'd not had the chance to get our newly recorded music out there, but we also knew this time would come. It was for us, the end of an era, fifteen years of rocking and rolling, with all the crazy capers that you've now read all about. The rest of us tried to continue the band but it wasn't the same, we needed a frontman, and so we decided that if we were to carry on in some way, we'd need to get a new lead singer and create a new band. We ended up doing just that, and not long after Tim left, Ste and I introduced Mark Hall to Sam and Luke, and we created a new band called Indianic***.

*Unfortunately, the Aire Do festival, which had lasted for nearly a decade ended in 2015.

**Harrison and Oliver later went on to form a band called The Veese. More info can be found in the Afterword section of this book.

***Indianic continued where The Undecided left off, writing new material, and performing at many pubs, music venues, and festivals until 2016.

A FAREWELL TO BOB

It was October 2011; we were in the Haworth Community Centre setting up for a band practice with Indianic when we learned some sad news from Sam. His dad had passed away in hospital after a short illness, he was only 63. Sam was distraught, and we did what we could to support him during this sad time. Bob Carlisle was quite well-known and a popular character in the Haworth and Keighley area. He was a university lecturer and linguist; he could speak maybe six or seven different languages fluently. He also had a love for music, and helped Sam back at the beginning, encouraging him to get the band going and helping us promote the gigs and compering at some of them too.

We were all gutted for Sam and knew it was a heavy blow for him as his dad was his mentor, his compass if you will, and although they didn't always see eye to eye, deep down they had massive love and respect for one another. Sam kept a brave face and stepped up, battled on, and decided to pay tribute to his dad by organising a farewell gig for him at the Parkside Club, as you know from reading this book, Bob was a loyal member of the club, it was his home from home.

Word had got around of Bobs passing, and it was in the Keighley News, who also paid tribute to him and mentioned the tribute gig which was to take place the day after his funeral. I remember arriving at the crematorium in Oakworth with my family and friends, there was a huge turnout for Bob, people came from far and wide to attend and pay their final respects.

The following evening was our turn to pay tribute to Bob, and the place was heaving. Sam had assembled a few bands he'd either played in or his dad had helped in the past. First up was The Undecided. Sam had called Tim and asked him if he'd come back and sing one more time, and he said, "It would be an honour to pay tribute to his dad". We played a handful of our well-known numbers to kick-start the show. Next up was a band called Snydes, who Sam and I both played for at the time, they were a popular covers band fronted by our mate Andrew 'Harry' Wilson from Haworth. After that, Sam and I were back on again playing with Indianic. We played what original songs we had at the time as we'd only been playing for a few months, and this was only our second live performance with an audience. Penultimately,

Sam's other band Wet Paint, played a bunch of their favourites. And finally, the headliners were The Culprits, who The Undecided had played alongside previously at The Guide Fest. They were also a band that Bob Carlisle had helped in their early days when he set up some jam nights at the Parkside Club. It was a great evening of music and one that Bob would have thoroughly approved of. Sam had done him proud to pull this together at such short notice, and to top it off we also managed to raise a few hundred pounds for Airedale Hospital's Intensive Care Unit which looked after Bob in his final days.

SIXTEEN DRUMMERS – THE STORY OF **THE UNDECIDED**

Bob and Kelly Carlisle – Parkside Club - 2008

SEE YOU ON THE OTHER SIDE

This has got to be the hardest story to write, it's the final story in the book, one I thought long and hard about for quite some time before putting on paper as its difficult to say things sometimes, but it's part of the story of The Undecided and as you'll probably agree, there's a main character to this book, to The Undecided as a band, to all the things we did, and crazy capers we got up to, that central character is Sam Carlisle. I wish he could be here today to share all these fantastic memories, I'm sure he would have told me a lot more stories, but maybe that'll come when we see him on the other side. XX

Following on from the tribute gig for Bob, we continued practising and gigging with Indianic, though it wasn't too long before the harsh reality of Bob no longer being around for Sam kicked in. He seemed to start losing his way, it was sad to see him like this. We tried our best to support him through these dark times, though it felt that his heart wasn't in the music anymore, he wasn't like he used to be. He did try, and continued to come to band practice sessions, but he seemed to struggle, and we all felt we couldn't continue like this. Ste and I said we'd have a word with Sam, and maybe ask him to have some time out from the band, but we didn't have the heart to do that and bottled it. Instead, Mark asked him to leave the band until a time he was ready to play again and take some time to sort himself out. But with Sam being Sam, he didn't take this well and pretty much fell out with us all, mainly me and Ste. After that, we didn't see or talk to each other for a few years.

It wasn't until New Year's Eve 2013 that I bumped into Sam at the Parkside Club. He didn't want to talk to me at first, telling me to go away, he had nothing to say. But I just wanted to say sorry, that's all. I spoke to his girlfriend JoJo, and she said he was pissed at me, but if I apologise and get him a drink, he'll probably want to chat. I bought him a pint and went and sat next to him and apologised, he started to feel more at ease. He did want to talk, but he was pissed off with me and Ste, his best mates who kind of betrayed him. He said, that if either one of us had asked him to leave the band, he would have understood, but because we coward out and let Mark ask him to leave, he was more upset with that, though he still deep down loved us both. We settled our differences and had a good night together chatting about some of the stories you've read in this book. It was sadly to be the very last time I spoke to Sam, his last words to me were, "Koe, I love ya mate, but you're a right boring bastard". I took that as a compliment, his ode back to me.

July 6th, 2014, sunny, clear blue skies. It was the 2nd leg of the Tour de France, and the route came right the way through Keighley, Haworth, and surrounding villages. I headed to Haworth to watch the spectacle with my family, and I must say it was the busiest I have ever seen in the village. There must have been 10's of thousands of people there all lining the route of the race. I saw many people I knew, but from a distance, this included Sam and his daughter walking towards the park. I couldn't say hello, I don't even think he noticed me, it was just heaving with crowds of people, and you couldn't move from one side of the road to the other for obvious reasons, so I found a spot to spectate at the bottom of Main Street and stayed put. *I didn't realise then; that it would be the very last time I would see Sam.* The race went by and from mine and my family's perspective, all was a good day, until we got home and heard the tragic news flooding in through social media.

Sam had collapsed outside the Parkside Club, which is where he was heading when I saw him earlier. He was rushed to hospital but passed away. I felt a crushing blow in my heart. I simply couldn't believe it, but it was confirmed by people who had been with him. How could this happen, he was only 36, I was devastated, completely numb, but for some reason, I held it all in, stayed as strong as I could, and my thoughts were with Sam's family, it must have been dreadful for them.

It wasn't until his funeral, that the realisation of not seeing Sam ever again crept up on me, but I held it in as best as I could. There was a huge turnout, just like with his dad Bob a few years earlier, all there to pay their final respects to a young lad they all knew and loved; someone that had become woven into the fabric of the Haworth community. It wasn't until I walked up to his coffin at the end of the service that I broke down in floods of tears. I've not cried like that since I was a little boy. I looked across at Tim and Steve and they too couldn't hold back the tears, we just needed to let it all out.

Afterwards, we all attended the wake which was held at the Parkside Club. People were reminiscing about the times they had with Sam, some of the stories you've read in this book were shared, and many others too, it was heartwarming to know so many people cared about him.

Not long after, came more sad news. Sam's younger brother Luke had also passed away, it was as though he couldn't continue without his dad or brother, it was such a tragic end. Life can be that way sometimes, happy, kind, fantastic and fun one minute, then so horribly cruel the next. All we are left with are the memories and stories of those who have come and gone. Hopefully, this book will serve as a time capsule of some of those great memories that can be handed down through the generations, and the story of The Undecided will continue for years to come.

SIXTEEN DRUMMERS – THE STORY OF **THE UNDECIDED**

Sam Carlisle – Parkside Club – 2008

SIXTEEN DRUMMERS – THE STORY OF **THE UNDECIDED**

APPENDICES

AFTERWORD

So, there you have it, the story of The Undecided, from humble beginnings in our youth, all the comings and goings and the highs and lows of life, the crazy capers we got up to, the friendships we made, up to the final chapter of saying goodbye to some of our closest friends. On reflection, we certainly had a good few years of fun, and we didn't half drink and smoke back then, proper carefree living, with a "world's your oyster" attitude. I'm glad we did what we did, granted, we didn't go all the way to stardom, but we were tryers and we did our bit for the local music scene and our loyal fans, and loved it all the same.

I guess you're thinking, what's next for The Undecided? Well, we have this book to promote, we want to get the story far and wide, so if you've enjoyed reading it, you too can also help us out by recommending it to others. As for performing our songs, you never know, we may end up jamming a few of our oldies now and again, so keep an eye on our Facebook page for future updates.

https://www.facebook.com/undecidedrockers

The above may also apply to Indianic.

https://www.facebook.com/indianicsounds

But to be honest, we've pretty much passed the baton to the younger generation. For instance, Ste's two lads Harrison and Oliver are now performing with their indie/pop/rock band The Veese, who could go all the way.

https://www.facebook.com/theveese

My nephew Charlie is the lead singer and guitarist in the grunge/rock band Stageminus and again, they too could be signed at any time, they're that good.

https://www.facebook.com/stageminus

My daughter Evie is a singer and musician, currently studying and performing music, and I'm sure she'll be one to watch in the future.

ON REFLECTION

A Special Bond

I never wanted to be in a band, I certainly didn't want to be a singer. I always loved music, and it played a big part in my life but the thought of standing in front of a crowd and singing was the last thing I wanted to do. Somehow, I started to sing in Sam's flat with him and Ste but that was just having a beer and a few songs, it was never going to be more.

Ste and Sam booked a gig at the Shoulder of Mutton and I really didn't want to do it but also I didn't want to let them down, so I went along with the thought that it would be probably the first and last gig...the performance was painfully embarrassing but the crowd was really busy and we got a kind of bamboozled but pleasant reaction so we felt quite good about it and even picked up a bass player from the performance.

Once Koe was onboard, we started to take it a bit more seriously and began to throw in some of our own songs. At that point, I was stuck and couldn't get out of it, but I was starting to think that we were actually starting to sound pretty good...there was a certain chemistry between the four of us but no drummer as yet. Once we found a drummer we started to gig quite often, and we were almost instantly followed by a really big crowd who continued to support us right to the end...we were so grateful for this that we were determined to make it worth their effort, and we rehearsed hard to get ourselves to a level to take it further.

Tempo injected some professionalism into us, and we were practising or gigging at least five days a week which led to us running a coach trip to watch us play at the world-famous Cavern in Liverpool...how did that happen from Sams flat to the Cavern in two years??? For the next few years, we were playing in iconic venues and meeting celebs here and there whilst going to the studio and recording music that I am still very proud of today.

With a little luck here and there and maybe a decision or two by us then I know that we would have moved up to the top level but The Undecided was a party where we got to do things that we could only dream about and got to do it with our mates and family, those days were magical and I thank everybody who came to watch and of course my fellow "Undies"...it's a special bond.

After reading Koe's book I am feeling happy that I was

part of the band. I have enjoyed reading an alternative version of the same things I did but seen from further back on stage. Koe and Ste were the hard-working part of the band, putting in so much time; Sam and I were less involved in the behind-the-scenes part. I think that we would have four very different books if we all wrote our own version of events...maybe only Koe would have a clear memory though.

Ste and I did radio interviews, and I did some on my own like Crash FM in Liverpool on the morning of one of the Cavern gigs. It was a fantastic way to spend my time and a great time in my life...forever an Undie. X

Tim Baldwin – September 2024

A great time, all of the time!

I'd like to thank Koe for all his efforts in The Undecided throughout the 90's and even more now, 30 years on for writing this book. Not to forget Jennie too, being married to me; a musician. A life of late nights, amps, guitars, pianos and drums scattered around each and every room of the house, accompanied by a regular noise of rehearsal and song writing for many years. This couldn't have been easy, but I think she handled it ok, well most of the time anyway xx

All our family and friends who jumped on the rollercoaster with us, big thank you. The ride wouldn't have been the same if we were sat in an empty carriage.

I've had the opportunity to write this reflection for a while now. I had to wait for the right time though, I feel the time is now. Let's be clear here, we were a pub band that did good. We were no global rock stars or even a UK massive. We were a bunch of working-class lads that moved out of the amateur rock n roll league and entered the "Vanarama division" of the football equivalent, maybe Division 2 at a push. But we did ok and progressed a little further than our local "K" Town venues.

It was 1994 and Sam Carlisle was one of my best mates, song writing partner, collaborator and sound board. The challenges we went through as young men with little money, later several children to think of and an absolute determination to succeed in life only helped us grow. To achieve something, anything, in order to get out of what we considered a place of limited opportunity and historical failings only drove us to further rant and collaborate with music, words and sound.

Koe and Tim had the same drive. As a four, our ambition, arrogance, and determination to not become a victim of the 90's northern employment struggle or fall foul to a lifetime of dirty foundry/factory work which poorly paid its workers was our aim. We wanted out, we were determined to make a change. We strived to do our best to influence our peers, avoid negative attitudes and travel whilst gigging and seeing new places. Luke Parker was the last member to join, he aligned with our ambition. He was the Sixteenth drummer, I always wished he was the first.

Some of the memories in this book I remember, some I don't. But what I do remember is that The Undecided had a great time all of the time and I'll never forget that time period in my life.

Whenever Sam and I were together and the night would come to an end, whilst walking away he'd turn around and say "Hey Ste! F###ing live forever man" …. then I'd shout it back. I didn't realise at the time the importance of our exchange of words, but now I know. In order to live forever you must always leave something behind………………….. I think we did.

Steven Houldsworth - September 2024

Warm Memories

"Wanna blast through of Don't Let Me Down by the Beatles?". I was 14 going on 15, upstairs at the British Legion in Haworth having an initial jam with Sam Carlisle. It was just the two of us for that jam, but it was the first time I had jammed with someone who I viewed as a seasoned gigging musician. I was nervous. Sam put me at ease. He was good like that. I was aware this was an informal audition to play with the Undecided and it felt like a pivotal moment in my formative stages of my musical career. I jammed with bands at school, but these were different. They had recorded EPs, had rows of gigs, played the Cavern! Also, my dad and brother knew of the band by being regulars at the Legion, so it all had the appearance of being "grown up", which flattered me. I relished it and was eager to get my teeth into learning their set. I loved playing gigs with them as the songs were so melodic and fun. Though my time with the band was brief, 20 plus years later I still remember a good chunk of the songs we played, have warm memories of the guys, singing solo McCartney tunes, talking about Cuba, and carrying forward musical lessons I learned (which were many).

Daniel Green – May 2024

Alongside and inside the Undecided.

When I was 16, I was in a band named Moondog. Because I had got to know Sam Carlisle through Jodie, my older sister. We were able to blag our way into supporting the Undecided at local venues such as the Parkside Social Club in Haworth, the Snooty Fox in Oakworth and many other places I can't recall off the top of my head, no doubt that list would include quite a few that sadly no longer exist. We also went along with the Undies to the Cavern Club in Liverpool on more than one occasion. For a young band, it was a great experience and an education in low level rock and roll excess.

By the beginning of 2002, I was now at the ripe old age of 19, Moondog had ceased to exist, and I was itching to start a band, so I and my good friends Charlie Smallwood and Sean Shackleton began rehearsing at the Musicians Centre which at the time was situated on the railway station bridge in Keighley. We soon realised that in order to make the amount of noise and feedback we required we would need another guitarist, so we approached Sam, and he agreed to join the band. This line up would go on to become known as Wet Paint and would have only a few years of drink fuelled and surprisingly creative madness before its inevitable implosion, but I can honestly say that it was some of the most fun I have had whilst being in a band. A lot of that due to Sam and the unpredictable hilarity that seemed to almost plague him.

I don't recall the exact dates, but I think it was sometime around 2008/2010 when the Undecided reformed after a long break. I was drafted into the band and would be the last in a suspiciously long line of drummers who had graced the stage with the Undies over the years. Although it would not be a great deal of time before the band finally broke up, I feel that 'Dance Like a Gecko,' our last EP recorded by Grant Henderson at IVOLV recording studio was some of the best work the Undecided did in terms of songwriting and musicianship. I am in no doubt that the appearance of a very special lady named Julie at the studio during the lead guitar takes will be well documented within the pages of this book, so I won't spoil it for you here.

I have been in a lot of bands and worked with a great deal of people over the last 30 years of being a musician, but some groups and individuals inevitably stand out from the rest. The Undecided were there from the beginning, they afforded us the opportunity to not only gig with them, but they were filling venues at the time, so we got the ear of a decent sized audience from very early on in our gigging career which I am grateful for. Ultimately by joining the band, I was also there to witness the end of an era in the Keighley music scene.

Rest in Peace Sam and I'll see you when I get there.

Luke Parker – September 2024

ACKNOWLEDGEMENTS

Writing this book has been a mammoth but worthy and rewarding task. It has brought back so many memories, some happy, and some sad, but all part of life's rich tapestry.

I want to thank those who helped contribute their memories to the book, Steve Houldsworth, Tim Baldwin, Scott Montgomery, Steve Tempest, Mark Tempest, Daniel Green, and Luke Parker.

I'd also like to thank my partner in crime Rachel Hickerton for all her hard work and effort with the fantastic illustrations throughout the book, and big thanks to Dean Baldwin for the fabulous cover design.

Mega thanks to John Robb for providing the Foreword, I am hugely grateful, and thanks to all our drummers named in this book; where would we have been without you?

Additional thanks go out to all those who supported The Undecided over the years, especially the girlfriends and wives of the band members who put up with all our antics, and big thanks to all my family and friends, those mentioned in this

book, and others. The list is too long, but you know who you are!

And finally, and not least, my thanks go out to family and friends who are sadly no longer with us, may you rest in peace, my thoughts are with you and your families.

RIP

Sam Carlisle, Bob Carlisle, Luke Carlisle, Kelly Carlisle, James Ackroyd, Nicholas Shepherd, Gareth Evans, Gordon 'Goose' Ahmadi, Martin Hardaker, Roy Farmer, Clement 'Clem' Holmes.

See you on the other side X

DISCOGRAPHY

Singles

2am

- 2am
- Happy Garden
- Brighter Day
- Real World

Burning/Feeling Better

- Burning
- Feeling Better
- Feeling Even Better (Feels like a house mix)

EP's

Strictly Rockers

- The Score
- Real World
- The Girl
- Rain or Shine
- 4-Track Dream
- Our Place

Dance Like a Gecko

- Dance Like a Gecko
- The Underclass
- I Will Get By
- Working Class Hero

Albums

Live May 98

- Like a Dove
- Feeling Better
- Absolute Madness
- Brighter Day
- Summer Song
- The Score
- Real World
- Our Place
- Summer Song (Pete's Remix)
- Absolute Madness (Acoustic Version)

Like a Dove

- Come Rain or Shine
- 4-Track Dream
- All Yours
- Not So Plain Jayne
- Pot of Gold
- Talkin' bout the Future
- Why You
- The Girl
- Absolute Madness
- Life's What You Make It
- Instrumental Mental

15 Years On And Still Rocking

- Dance Like a Gecko
- Green Mile (Live)
- The Underclass
- I Will Get By
- Working Class Hero
- Merry-go-round (Live)
- Dynamite Shed (Live)
- Happy Garden (Reprise)

All songs can be found on SoundCloud at the following link:

https://soundcloud.com/user-191071063

GIGOGRAPHY

1996

- April - The Shoulder of Mutton – Thwaites Village, Keighley
- May - The Tap & Spile – Harrogate
- July - The Shoulder of Mutton – Thwaites Village, Keighley
- Aug - The Druids Arms – Long Lee, Keighley
- Nov 30th - Conservative Club – Wilsden, Bradford
- December - The Druids Arms – Long Lee, Keighley

1997

- Feb 1st - The Druids Arms – Long Lee, Keighley
- Feb 12th - The Fleece Inn - Haworth
- Feb 16th - Shoulder of Mutton – Thwaites Village, Keighley
- Feb 26th - The Fleece Inn – Haworth
- Mar 20th - The Hospital Social Club – Harrogate
- Apr 4th - The Druids Arms – Long Lee, Keighley
- Apr 18th - The Victoria Lodge – Birkenhead
- May 9th - The Royal Oak, Keighley
- May 23rd - Kings Head – Keighley
- May 30th - The White Bear – Eastburn
- Jun 3rd - Queens Hall – Bradford
- Jun 6th - Kings Head – Keighley
- Jun 13th - The British Legion – Haworth
- Jun 20th - The Druids Arms – Long Lee, Keighley
- Jul 16th - The Punch Bowl – Silsden
- Sep 12th - The Druids Arms – Long Lee, Keighley
- Sep 26th - The White Bear – Eastburn
- Oct 3rd - The Victoria Hotel – Keighley
- Oct 11th - Robbo's - Thwaites Village, Keighley
- Oct 27th - The White Bear - Eastburn
- Dec 26th - Robbo's - Thwaites Village, Keighley
- Dec 31st - The British Legion – Haworth

1998

- Jan 10th - The Three Horses - Keighley
- Jan 30th - The Druids Arms – Long Lee, Keighley
- May 15th - The Fenton – Leeds

- May 22nd - The White Bear – Eastburn
- May 23rd - The British Legion – Haworth
- May 25th - The Cavern Club – Liverpool
- Jun 10th - The Victoria Hotel – Keighley
- Jun 11th - The Snooty Fox – Oakworth
- Aug 22nd - Boothy's – Keighley
- Aug 28th - The Picket – Liverpool
- Aug 29th - The Cavern Club – Liverpool
- Sep 4th - The British Legion – Haworth
- Sep 11th - The Harrogate Arms – Harrogate
- Sep 24th - The Globe – Keighley
- Sep 25th - The Pop & Pasty Social Club - Keighley
- Oct 29th - The Druids Arms – Long Lee, Keighley
- Nov 7th - The British Legion – Haworth
- Nov 13th - The Pop & Pasty Social Club – Keighley
- Nov 14th - Royal Park – Leeds
- Nov 19th - The Trades Club – Hebden Bridge
- Nov 20th - The Fenton – Leeds
- Nov 21st - The Golden Eagle - Leeds
- Nov 28th - The Cavern Club – Liverpool
- Nov 29th - The Pogue Mahone – Liverpool
- Dec 26th - The British Legion - Haworth

1999

- Jan 30th - The Craven Pub – Skipton
- Feb 12th - The Trades Club – Hebden Bridge (supporting HMHB)
- Feb 27th - The Cavern Club – Liverpool
- Mar 27th - The British Legion - Haworth
- Apr 5th - The Cavern Club – Liverpool
- Jun 16th - Victoria Hall – Keighley (Keighley Festival)
- Jun 18th - The Duchess – Leeds
- June - Party at the manor (date unknown)
- Jul 3rd - The Craven Pub – Skipton
- Jul 8th - The Snooty Fox – Oakworth
- Jul 16th - The British Legion – Haworth
- Jul 31st - The Cheese 'n' Trumpet – Keighley
- Oct 30th - The Cheese 'n' Trumpet – Keighley
- Nov 26th - The Ferrands Arms – Bingley
- Nov 27th - Victoria Hall – Keighley (Vinyl Dreamz)
- Dec 11th - The Cavern Club – Liverpool

2000

- Aug 18th - The British Legion – Haworth (Arts Festival)
- Oct 13th - The British Legion – Haworth

2001

- Feb 24th - The Martins Nest – Brighouse
- Apr 19th - The Roadhouse – Manchester

2002

- Jul 20th - The Parkside Club – Haworth

2003

- Apr 19th - The Parkside Club – Haworth
- School gig – (unknown School) - Bradford

2004

- Jul 17th - The Guide Inn – Cullingworth, Keighley (Guide Fest)

2009

- Jul 3rd - Beat-Herder Festival – Ribble Valley
- August - The Sun Pub - Lepton, Huddersfield (date unknown)
- Nov 14th - The Parkside Club – Haworth
- Nov 20th - The Druids Arms – Long Lee, Keighley
- Nov 21st - Keighley Cricket Club – Keighley

2010

- Jul 17th - Cliffe Castle Park – Keighley (The Aire Do)
- Aug 29th - Bradford & Bingley Rugby Club, Bingley (Acoustic gig)

2011

- Oct 15th - Parkside Club – Haworth (Bob Carlisle Benefit Gig)

SUPPORT BANDS

Over the years, we have had the privilege of playing alongside many bands. Some supported us, we supported some of them, and some were on the same bill as us at various gigs, festivals, and events. Here's a list of all of those I can remember.

FIFA Guppy **Circus?** Fire **Moondog** Montauk Island **The Pipers** Dead Celebs **Operator 6** Box Jellys **Wet Paint** Fifteen Stories **Random Hand** Lord Ryan and the Tops **Johnny and the Poorboys** Snydes **Indianic** Powder Monkeys **Skeletal Family** Cosmic Cuppa **Resin** Mother Goose **Half Man Half Biscuit** Halo Czars **Clipper Cartel** Zero **Reverend and the Makers** Cacophonix **Insense** Euphony **Happy Accident** Jupiter **Nameless** Scratch **Cream River** Surface **Waste of Space** Moon Boogie **Claude Sword** Abyss **52 Teenagers** Precinct **Nexus** No Home UK **The Culprits** Ironstorm **Angel Chain** Kinesis **Aspire** 3 Men and a Bass **Captain Hotknives** Hollow Horse **The Big Bang** Eponymouse **Howling Johnny & The Full Moon Blues Band** The Lajpal Group (UK) **Meet The Committee** Revolver **Father Hen** Arcomnia **Meet Me In Vegas** Delorean Drivers **Lovely Eggs**

GEAR

We used a mix of guitars, amps, and auxiliaries, which I've referenced throughout this book as 'Gear', so here's a list of what we used over the years.

Guitars

- Washburn D15 Acoustic Guitar
- Epiphone (Hofner style) Violin Bass
- Fender Precision Bass
- Epiphone Rivoli Bass
- Washburn J21CE EQ400 Acoustic Guitar
- Rickenbacker 325 reproduction
- Epiphone SG Black
- Epiphone Sheraton (on loan from Noel Gallagher)
- Epiphone SG Burgandy
- Tanglewood Indiana TW28ST
- Fender 12 String

Amps

- Marshall 2x12 Combo Amp
- Vox 2x12 Combo Amp
- Trace Elliot Commando 12 Combo Bass Amp
- Trace Elliot AH300 & 4 x 10 Cab Bass Amp
- Laney VC30 2x12 Combo Amp
- Cig packet Amp

PA & Auxiliaries

- The mighty FAL
- Peavey XR600E with Eurosys 2 x 12 Cabs
- Torque TM100P Powered Monitor
- Beyer TG-X180 Microphone
- Shure 57 Microphone (on loan from Liam Gallagher)
- Multiple Pedals
- Tambourine
- Drum kits x 16

If you purchased this book on Amazon, please don't forget to leave a review/rating. *****

Alternatively, you can email **16drummers@gmail.com**

or post on the book's Facebook page
https://www.facebook.com/sixteendrummers

More illustrations and artwork can be found at the following link.

https://www.facebook.com/rachelhickertonillustrations

Thank you!

INDEX

A

Abyss, - 260 -
Adam Shepherd, - 203 -
Alex McKechnie, -90 -, - 94 -, - 106 -
Andrew 'Harry' Wilson, - 230 -
Andy 'Easty' Eastwood, - 106, - 139 -
Andy Pendle, - 165 -
Andy Turner, - 138 -
Angel Chain, - 209 -, - 260 -
Aphex Twin, - 171 -
Arcomnia, - 227 -, - 260 -
Artimesia, - 197 -
Aspire, - 157 -, - 260 -
Austin Powers, - 47 -
Autechre, - 171 -

B

Badly Drawn Boy, - 180 -, - 181 -
Barcode, - 197 -, - 202 -
Baz Cooper, - 31 -
Barry 'Baz' Houldsworth, - 57 -, - 58 -, - 110 -
BBC Radio 6 Music, - 211 -
BCB Radio, - 114 -, - 123 -
Beat-Herder Festival, - 77 -, - 214 -, - 215 -, - 218 -, - 225 - , - 259 -
Ben Furness, - 45 -
Bez, - 181 -, - 183 -, - 184 -
Billy Duffy, - 205 -

Bingley Music Live, - 208 -
Bloodstream, - 202 -
Blur, - 60 -, - 151 -
Boards of Canada, - 171 -
Bob Carlisle, - 78 -, - 79 -, - 80 -, - 96 -, - 229 -, - 230 -, - 231 -, - 232 -, - 233 -, - 236 -, - 254 -, - 259 -
Bob Hardaker, - 24 -
Bonehead (Paul Arthurs), - 14 -, - 204 -
Bottom, - 174 -
Box Jellys, - 226 -, - 260 -
Buzzcocks, - 95 -, - 146 -, - 177 -

C

Cacophonix, - 260 -
Captain Hotknives, - 216 -, - 260 -
Carl Stipetic, - 16 -, - 139 -, - 169 -
Cast, - 81 -, - 82 -
Cavern Club, - 15 -, - 90 -, - 93 -, - 94 -, - 95 -, - 96 -, - 97 -, - 98 -, - 99 -, - 100 -, - 102 -, - 106 -, - 108 -, - 114 -, - 115 -, - 133 -, - 134 -, - 157 -, - 171 -, - 244 -, - 245 -, - 249 -, - 250 -, - 258 -
Charlie Ousey, - 242 -
Charlie Smallwood, - 140 -, - 250 -
Chris Jackson, - 16 -, - 36 -, - 40 -
Chris Jessop. - 131 -
Chris 'Skoony' Myerscough, - 40 -, - 95 -, - 138 -
Chuck Berry, - 28 -
Circus?, - 197 -, - 198 -, - 202 -, - 204 -, - 209 -, - 260 -
Claude Sword, - 260 -
Clement 'Clem' Holmes, - 254 -
Clipper Cartel, - 260 -

Coldplay, - 159 -, - 160 -, - 194 -
Colonel Decker, - 56 -
Cornershop, - 82 -
Cosmic Cuppa, - 202 -, - 203 -, - 260 -
Courtney Love, - 85 -
Cream River, - 260 -

D

Damon Gough, - 180 -, - 181 -, - 183 -, - 187 -, -188 -
Daniel Green, - 2 -, - 16 -, - 141 -, - 211 -, - 249 -, - 253 -
Danny Kenealy, - 138 -
Danny Wood, - 138 -
David Anderton, - 140 -
David Barnett, - 53 -
David Gilmour, - 101 -
David Knights, - 53 -, - 90 -, - 193 -
Dead Celebs, - 260 -
Dead Men Walking, - 205 -
Deaf School, - 110 -
Dean Baldwin, - 2 -, - 59 -, - 63 -, - 134 -, - 154 -, - 155 -, - 171 -, - 253 -
Debbie Magee, - 214 -
Deepfill, - 197 -
Def Leppard, - 219 -
DeLorean Drivers, - 227 -, - 260 -
DJ Tempest, - 197 -
Donald Ward, - 105 -
Dynamo, - 206 -

E

Echo and The Bunnymen, - 85 -
Eddie Hitler, - 174 -
Elbow, - 194 -
Emma Baylin, - 76 -, - 77 -, - 138 -
Ennio Morricone, - 199 -
Episonic, - 197 -
Eponymous, - 157 -, - 260 -
Euphony, - 158 -, - 260 -
Evie Shepherd, - 225 -, - 242 -

F

Fake Uzi, - 197 -
Father Hen, - 227 -, - 260 -
FIFA Guppy, - 74 -, - 77 -, - 260 -
Fifteen Stories, - 227 -, - 260 -
52 Teenagers, - 260 -
Fire, - 99 -, - 260 -
Fluke Shot Frenzy, - 197 -, - 202 -
For a Few Dollars More, - 190 -, - 195 -
Foxes Faux, - 227 -
Frank Sidebottom, - 188 -
Frank Sinatra, - 76 -
Fugoo, - 202 -

G

Gareth Evans, - 66 -, - 67 -, - 68 -, - 69-, - 254 -
Gareth Gates, - 206 -
Gary 'Rocky' Dwyer, - 16 -, - 139 -

Geoff The Chauffeur, - 43 -, - 45 -, - 47 -, - 50 -, - 55 -, - 56 -, - 65 -
Get Guns, - 211 -
Glen Matlock, - 205 -
Gordon 'Goose' Ahmadi, -138 -, - 254 -
Graham Fletcher, - 50 -, - 71 -
Grant Henderson, - 222 -, - 251 -
Gregg Lewis, - 16 -, - 191 -, - 192 -, - 194 -, - 195 -
Guide Fest, - 140 -, - 208 -, - 211 -, - 231 -, - 259 -
Guigsy (Paul McGuigan), - 14 -

H

Half Man Half Biscuit, - 109 -, - 110 -, - 111 -, - 260 -
Halo Czars, - 260 -
Happy Accident, - 260 -
Hard City Records, - 105 -, - 107 -
Harrison Houldsworth, - 140 -, - 225 -, - 228 -, - 242 -
Heather Clapham, - 59 -, - 62 -, - 63 -, - 154 -, - 155 -
Hollow Horse, - 157 -, - 260 -
Howling' Johnny and The Full Moon Blues Band, - 227 -, - 260 -
Hush, - 197 -, - 202 -
Huw Stephens, - 211 -

I

Ian 'Scouse' Clarke, - 108 -
Ill Bass Method, - 222 -
In A City studio, - 169 -, - 195 -
Indianic, - 217 -, - 227 -, - 228 -, - 229 -, - 230 -, - 233 -, - 242 -, - 260 -

Insense, - 152 -, - 260 -
Ironstorm, - 202 -, - 260 -

J

Jaine Wood, - 138 -
Jake Bugg, - 227 -
James 'Aky' Ackroyd, - 16 -, - 87 -,- 89 -, - 97 -, - 103 - - 139 -, - 254 -
James Redmond, - 177 -, - 180 -
Jason Rhodes, - 172 -, - 175 -, - 186 -, - 204 -
Jennie Houldsworth, - 138 -, - 180 -, - 246 -
Jim Turner, - 105 -
Joe McKechnie, - 106
Joe Strummer, - 11 -
Joe Woodger, - 16 -, - 36 -
John Gow, - 157 -
John Lennon, - 95 -, - 98 -, - 224 -
John Peel, - 109 -
John Robb, - 11 -, - 177 -, - 183 -, - 187 -, - 189 -, - 253 -
John Shuttleworth, - 30 -
John Sullivan, - 3 -
John Squire, - 182 -
Johnny and the Poorboys, - 157 -, - 197 -, - 202 -, - 260 -
Jonathan Dunn, - 133 -
Jupiter, - 260 -

K

Kasabian, - 160 -
Kelly Carlisle, - 232 -, - 254 -
Keighley Albion RLFC, - 57 -, - 58 -
Keighley News, - 51 -, - 53 -, - 90 -, - 193 -, - 230 -

Kief Lloyd, - 197 -
Kinesis, - 157 -, - 260 -
Kirk Brandon, - 205 -
Kurt Cobain, - 14 -

L

Lee Bilbrough, - 181 -, - 182 -
Lewie Shepherd, - 144 -, - 225 -
Lewis T, - 165 -
Liam Gallagher, - 14 -, - 174 -, - 181, - 182 -, - 184 -, - 261 -
Lionel Skerratt, - 16 -, - 139 -, - 153 -, - 154 -, - 171 -
Lord Ryan and the Tops, - 260 -
Louder Than War, - 187 -
Lovely Eggs, - 227 -, - 260 -
Luke Matthews, - 16 -, - 42 -, - 44 -, - 46 -, - 59 -, - 61 -, - 62 -, - 63 -, - 75 -, - 86 -, - 87 -, - 139 -
Luke Parker, - 2 -, - 16 -, - 99 -, - 139 -, - 214 -, - 214 -, - 218 , - 219 -, - 220 -, - 221-, - 227 -, 237 -, - 247 -, - 252 -, - 253 -

M

Manic Street Preachers, - 158 -
Marie Shepherd, - 100 -, - 136 -
Mark Hall, - 215 -, - 217 -, - 227 -, - 234 -
Mark 'Daggy' Tempest, - 2 -, - 146 -, - 151 -, - 253 -
Martin Hardaker, - 24 -, - 254 -
Meet Me in Vegas, - 227 -, - 260 -
Meet the Committee, - 227 -, - 260 -
Michael 'Boy' Reddiough, - 206 -

Mick Baker, - 44 -, - 73 -, - 74 -
Mickey Waddington, - 140 -
Mick Jagger, - 183 -
Mike Bower, - 106 -
Mike Joyce, - 204 -
Mike Peters, - 205 -
Mill Studio, - 71 -, - 78 -
Molly Ousey, - 140 -
Montauk Island, - 197 -, - 202 -, - 260 -
Moon Boogie, - 260 -
Moondog, - 99 -, - 157 -, - 250 -, - 260 -
Mother Goose, - 260 -
Muse, - 194 -
M-Zone, - 165 -

N

Nameless, - 260 -
Neil Crossley, - 109 -
Nexus, - 209 -, - 260 -
Nicholas Shepherd, - 12 -, - 191 -, - 207 -, - 254 -
Nick Chambers, - 77 -
Nigel Blackwell, - 109 -
Nirvana, - 14 -, - 24 -, - 158 -, - 198 -
No Home UK, - 260 -
Noel Gallagher, - 14 -, - 172 -, - 181 -, - 261 -
Nudge, - 61 -

O

Oasis, - 11 -, - 14 -, - 15 -, - 24 -, - 45 -, - 81 -, - 82 -, - 158 -, - 171 -, - 174 -, - 181 -, - 182 -, - 187 -, - 188 -, - 204 -, - 206 -
Ocean Colour Scene, - 206 -
Oliver Houldsworth, - 225 -, - 228 -, - 242 -
Operator 6, - 202 -, - 203 -, - 206 -, - 260 -
Only Fools and Horses, - 92 -

P

Patsy Kensit, - 182 -
Paul Allen, - 138 -
Paul Calf, - 183 -
Paul McCartney, - 34 -, - 98 -, - 100 -, - 101 -, -249 -
Paul Weller, - 206 -
Pearl Jam, - 65 -
Pete Shepherd, - 133 -, - 222 -
Pink Floyd, - 58 -, - 101 -
Pocketsize, - 202 -
Pogue Mahone, - 100 -, - 114 -, - 258 -
Powder Monkeys, - 202 -, - 204 -, - 260 -
Precinct, - 260 -
Princess Anne, - 44 -
Pulp, - 65 -

Q

Queens Hall, - 65 -, - 68 -, - 69 -, - 91 -, - 257 -

R

Rachel Auburn, - 165 -
Rachel Hickerton, - 2 -, - 253 -, - 262 -
Random Hand, - 209 -, - 260 -
Reebok Stadium, - 172 -, - 174 -, - 184 -
Resin, - 158 -, - 260 -
Reverend and The Makers, - 227 -, - 260 -
Revolver, - 227 -, - 260 -
Ritchie Valens, - 28 -
Rob Jones, - 180 -
Robert Carlyle, - 107 -
Robert Harvey, - 159 -
Rockbottom Risers, - 227 -
Roger Nowell, - 204 -
Ronald Koeman, - 159 -
Rowetta, - 183 -
Roy Farmer, - 200 -, - 201 -, - 254 -
Rudimental, - 227 -

S

S.A.M Acoustics, - 24 -, - 34 -
Sam Houldsworth, - 44 -
Sam Shepherd, - 68 -, - 133 -, - 138 -
Samuel L Jackson, - 107 -
Sarah Butterfield, - 138 -
Schrödinger's Cat, - 197 -, - 202 -
Scott 'Monty' Montgomery, - 2 -, - 21 -, - 23 -, - 26 -, - 27 -, - 38 -, - 213 -, - 253 -
Scratch, - 260 -
Sean Shackleton, - 140 -, - 250 -

Sergio Leone, - 199 -
Sharon Anderson, - 138 -
Shaun Ryder, - 181 -, - 183 -, - 184 -
Simon Ashberry, - 53 -
Simon 'Simi' Waddington, - 29 -, - 32 -, - 33 -
Simon Cartwright, - 16 -, - 34 -, - 91 -
Simon Rook, - 140 -
Skeletal Family, - 202 -, - 204 -, - 205 -, - 260 -
Slider, - 197 -
Snydes, - 230 -, - 260 -
Spear of Destiny, - 205 -
Spinal Tap, - 121 -
Stageminus, - 242 -
Stan Greenwood, - 204 -
Stephen 'Smiggy' Smith, - 140 -, - 209 -
Steve Smith, - 16 -, - 102 -, - 103 - , - 104 -, - 105 -, - 107 -, - 128 -, - 134 -, - 135 -, - 136 -, - 137 -, - 138 -, - 139 -
Stonefish, - 197 -, - 202 -
Sue Burke, - 138 -
Sue Ryder Manorlands Hospice, - 44 -, - 197 -, - 200 -, - 209 -
Suede, - 5 -
Surface, - 77 -, - 260 -

T

Tess Daly, - 180 -
Telegraph & Argus, - 51 -, - 53 -
Tha Operator, - 202 -
The Adventures of B Violet, - 202 -
The Aire Do, - 144 -, - 225 -, - 227 -, - 228 -, - 259 -

The Alarm, - 205 -
The A-Team, - 56 -
The Beatles, - 15 -, - 24 -, - 33 -, - 34 -, - 81 -, - 82 -, - 90 -, - 92 -, - 95 -, - 98 -, - 206 -, - 249 -
The Big Bang, - 157 -, - 260 -
The Clash, - 95 -, - 146 -
The Cranberries, - 65 -
The Culprits, - 208 -, - 209 -, - 231 -, - 260 -
The Cult, - 205 -
The Damned, - 146 -
The Dogs, - 204 -
The Duchess, - 158 -, - 160 -, - 194 -, - 258 -
The La's, - 81 -
The Lajpal Group (UK), - 227 -, - 260 -
The Membranes, - 178 -
The Picket, - 100 -, - 106 -, - 114 -, - 137 -, - 258 -
The Pipers, - 108 -, - 202 -, - 260 -
The Roadhouse, - 194 -, - 259 -
The Rolling Stones, - 24 -, - 28 -, - 82 -
The Sex Pistols, - 76 -, - 95 -, - 146 -, - 205 -
The Smiths, - 204 -
The Stone Roses, - 178 -, - 182 -
The Stranglers, - 95 -
The Teardrop Explodes, - 16 -, - 85 -
The Trades Club, - 108 -, - 109 -, - 194 -, - 258 -
The Veese, - 228 -, - 242 -
The Verve, - 45 -, - 81 -, - 82 -, - 158 -
The White Stripes, - 194 -
The Queen, - 40 -, - 42 -
3 Men and a Bass, - 157 -, - 260 -
Threshold Shift, - 202 -

Thunderbirds, - 45 -
Timothy Taylor's, - 23 -, - 118 -
Tony Leighton, - 158 -, - 159 -
Tony McCarroll, - 14 -
Tony Ousey, - 140 -

V

Vernon Kay, - 173 -
Vinne & The Stars, - 222 -
Vinyl Dreamz, - 165 -, - 258 -

W

Waste of Space, - 252 -
Western Suburbs, - 194 -, - 197 -, - 202 -
Wet Paint, - 195 -, - 198 -, - 202 -, - 204 -, - 208 -, - 211 -, - 213 -, - 231 -, - 250 -, - 260 -

Z

Zero, - 260 -

The End

Printed in Great Britain
by Amazon